ITI CONFERENCE 2

Translators and Interpreters Mean Business

ITI CONFERENCE 2

Translators and Interpreters Mean Business

Edited by
Catriona Picken

Proceedings of the second annual conference of the
Institute of Translation and Interpreting

29–30 April 1988
Hotel Russell, London

First published in 1988
by Aslib, The Association for Information Management
Information House
26-27 Boswell Street
London WC1N 3JZ

© Aslib and contributors, 1988

All rights reserved

British Library Cataloguing in Publication Data

Institute of Translation and Interpretation,
    Conference (2nd: 1988: London)
    ITI Conference 2: translators and
    interpreters mean business
    1. Languages.   Translation
    I. Title   II. Picken, Catriona, *1934–*
    418'.02

ISBN 0-85142-240-3

Printed and bound in Great Britain by
Biddles Limited, Guildford, Surrey

Contents

Conference Committee

Jean Kirby (Chairman)
Dr Marie-Josée Andreasen
David Beattie
Roger Fletcher
John Gardam
Hugh Keith
Valerie Landon
Pamela Mayorcas
Mike Shields
Jane Taylor
Albin Tybulewicz
Hilde Watson
Dimity Castellano (Secretary)

Introduction

Catriona Picken

This book gives an account of the second international conference and exhibition of the Institute of Translation and Interpreting*, held at the same venue and the same time of year as the first. The mixture was also roughly the same as before, with sessions on a particular theme being followed by open discussion on the topics presented, and an even more open discussion at the two forums on the second day, one for translators and one for interpreters.

The overall theme this year was 'Translators and Interpreters Mean Business' and it was therefore appropriate that the conference should be launched by Michael Forrest of ICL, i.e. from the world of (very big) business. Nowadays every business with aspirations to become really sizeable must participate fully in the international market, and the first three papers illustrated this point. Alan Gilderson gave an account of the marketing of products which are not bought by the man in the street (e.g. nuclear-powered icebreakers), but are sold, probably in small numbers, to organisations which might be located anywhere in the world. Despite having once lived in the house of Dr Zamenhof, Valerie Landon, the next speaker, realised that Esperanto is not the solution to all our problems, and became an interpreter. One of her difficulties, however, is that not all businesses in the United Kingdom are fully aware of what a properly qualified interpreter can do for them. The third speaker in this first session, John Seager of Duracell batteries (an international product if ever there was one) concentrated on the aspect of manufacturing in various countries.

Lunch on the first day was enlivened by a light-hearted talk from John D. Graham, which I am glad to be able to present to readers along with the other more serious items. It is just these more informal parts of a conference which are usually missing from the published *Proceedings*.

The papers at the second session, which was entitled 'Technology', gave an account of two of the kinds of technology now available for translators and interpreters – for those in the European Community organisations, Chris Burdon described the creation and progress of the Council of Ministers termbank, and Dr Keith Adkins gave valuable guidance on how translators can start to find their way through the maze of word processing systems currently available on the market.

*ITI, 318a Finchley Road, London NW3 5HT. Telephone: 01-794 9931 (+44 1 794 9931).

The last session on the first day covered three different aspects of training: Michael Croft described the postgraduate course at Bath, one of the earliest in the field in the United Kingdom. Next, Alastair Scouller gave an account of how at least some of the community interpreters in England are trained. The main feature here is that the trainees are not professional linguists and their training has to be tackled in a very practical way. To end the session, Heinrich Allissat talked about the novel system of on-the-job training for new translators used at Krupps in Germany.

The first session on the following day started with Professor Danica Seleskovitch discussing the theory of translation as put into practice at her institution, the Ecole Supérieure d'Interprètes et de Traducteurs in Paris, followed by Robert David MacDonald's paper on the dramatic translator. Readers of the *Proceedings* will no doubt be disappointed to discover that we have no full text for this paper, which was in the nature of an ad hoc virtuoso performance. The pitfalls and problems of scientific translation were described by E. Boris Uvarov, with expert guidance on how to avoid and/or overcome them.

The conference next turned its attention to interpreting. During this session, Christiane Driesen gave a vivid account of the realities of court interpreting in the Federal Republic of Germany, and Liese Katschinka, as a member of the FIT Interpreters' Committee, gave a more general view of the interpreting world, together with her thoughts on what the future may hold.

For the final two sessions, the Translators' Forum and the Interpreters' Forum, the idea was to have as wide-ranging a discussion as possible, with active participation by conference delegates. The translators were presented with food for thought and a range of topics for discussion by Charles Polley, the session chairman, followed by two speakers from opposite sides of the English Channel (or La Manche) on how they go about their business. These papers, by Lanna Castellano and Florence Herbulot are reproduced here. It will perhaps not come as a surprise to readers of the *Proceedings* to learn that the presentations at the Interpreters' Forum have not come down to us in written form, but I can at least offer an excellent summary of the whole discussion by Helena Bayliss.

These two forums, followed by Patricia Crampton's summing-up, brought the formal business of the conference to a close. The Annual General Meeting of the ITI, held the next day, was gratifyingly well attended too, and I understand that the intention is follow much the same pattern next year.

A conference of this kind has to fulfil many functions, one of which, and in my view a very important one, is to give the conference participants a chance to meet each other and exchange views. This was the idea behind the dozen or so 'parallel sessions' which took place all over the Hotel Russell at the same time as the two forums. But it meant that decisions had to be made – did one attend just one parallel session, e.g. the Italian network's, or circulate round them in case one was missing something vital at, say, the East Anglia Regional

Group get-together? All the participants had to make up their own mind and I am sure it was not easy. We look forward to getting reactions from the participants to this and other features of the Conference.

Having said that, there is no denying that the whole two days went very well, due in no small measure to the thorough work done by the organising committee and secretariat, plus the invaluable cooperation of the Hotel Russell staff. The exhibitors are always welcome visitors to the conference, providing information and demonstrations with unfailing zest. More than one person has commented on the vital role of the stewards, recruited from a variety of universities, etc. I hope that the stewards too derive benefit from their contacts with the conference participants. Finally, as always, I must pay tribute to the rapporteurs. Their discussion reports are much appreciated by readers of the *Proceedings*, and rightly so. Their task is not an easy one, but they perform it efficiently and above all willingly! My grateful thanks to them all.

This Introduction has already referred to the plans for next year. For those of us in Europe (and elsewhere) the next few years are the run-up to the Single European Market to be launched in 1992, and I have no doubt that future ITI conferences will take this fully into account. But once the Single European Market is in being, it will not then go away. The role of the ITI and of translators and interpreters in general will, we all hope, be just as vital, if not more so, in the years after 1992.

Opening remarks

Juan Sager

President, ITI

Welcome to this second international conference of the Institute of Translation and Interpreting. On this second occasion we have a record attendance of nearly 300 participants with visitors from Australia, Austria, Belgium, France, the Federal Republic of Germany, Iraq, Ireland, Italy, The Netherlands, Norway, Spain, Sweden, the People's Republic of Yemen and the United States of America.

This impressive response to a professional meeting, for once not dedicated to highlighting the blessings of information technology, is a reflection of the growing self-awareness and unity of a profession which for too long has been beset by doubts and divisions harmful both to its external image and its internal cohesion. It is therefore also a matter of pride for me to announce here that the membership of the Institute of Translation and Interpreting has also grown over the last year and now stands at 870 members.

Last year we met under the motto 'The Business of Translation and Interpreting' and gave an overview of the current state of the art of the profession. I think we demonstrated on that first public occasion of the Institute that the business of translation is increasingly computer-based and that this business is diversifying to include writing, editing and even publishing as well as the organisation of conferences and language planning.

The theme of this year's conference is 'Translators and Interpreters Mean Business'. If I may be permitted to paraphrase this motto I can identify two complementary meanings. By facilitating communication across linguistic barriers, translators and interpreters mean, or better represent, a lot of business opportunities for people who need our skills. We also mean business in the sense that we are serious about the quality of our work and the standards of service we provide.

Let me briefly illustrate what I mean by a little story told me by a senior translation manager in one of the European Community departments. One evening he received a document which was the result of many hours of drafting by officials who had all agreed to use French as a working language. This document was required in the other eight official Community languages by the next afternoon. You will know that Community documents after translation become fully equivalent texts for all purposes of national usage and that such multilingual documents then can become subjects of official communiqués or be published in the multilingual *Journal officiel*. This is not an uncommon request. My friend examined the document and said that he could not provide a translation in time because he doubted whether his translators could understand it sufficiently well to provide eight versions which could be said to be fully equivalent. He could, however, see a way out of the difficulty, if he could first rewrite this result of multilingual compromise in monolingual French. Once he had a clear source text, he said, he could then deliver translations into eight other languages in a matter of a few hours. The offer was accepted and the committee that was responsible for the original draft was delighted with the result. The translations were provided in time and everybody lived happily ever after. And the moral of this anecdote is: Translators are writers, who can only produce when they have a clear text in front of them. If they do not, they must intervene in the writing process.

This is just one example of the way we can assist the business of communication. This conference will provide many other ways in which translators and interpreters mean business.

Keynote address

Michael Forrest

ICL Europe, London, UK

The theme of this conference 'Translators and Interpreters Mean Business', is dear to my own concerns as a businessman in a truly international business. The information technology business (I am old enough to remember it being called 'the computer business') is indeed truly international. Competition in it flows across national boundaries to probably a greater extent than any other industry.

My own company ICL, for instance, operates in over seventy countries, including, of course, all those of the European Community. It is a major part of the STC Group which is the fourth largest electronics group in Europe. Equally, the importance of language does not escape us. (In the computer business we tend to call it 'natural language' to distinguish the real thing from our computer languages like COBOL, FORTRAN, PASCAL, C and other more or less exotically named fabrications.)

For UK industry as a whole, less than one quarter of total exports go to English-speaking countries. It is frequently pointed out that English has widespread use as a 'business' language. But the fact of the matter is that not to sell in the language of the purchaser is a competitive disadvantage that takes a lot of offsetting by better product or service. It is a very arrogant company that thinks it has a divine right to such offsetting competitive advantage.

My company has over 5,500 people outside the United Kingdom, nearly 30 per cent of its total staff, and only about 200 of these are expatriate British. The management of our operating companies outside the United Kingdom is very largely composed of nationals of those countries, at the highest level almost universally so. As a result, the language dimension is more an internal matter than a hindrance to our relations with our customers.

However, now that to an ever greater extent information technology handles text rather than predominantly figures, the language issues are growing apace in the product's specification and design. We used to think software was difficult enough to get right in one language. Now it has to be in many, so that business solutions rather than hardware have become what the IT industry offers to its users. These solutions have to be truly in the 'business culture' and the language of the user, and not just in Japanese handbook English (or menu French). Furthermore, on this important theme of language in the product, the IT solution is increasingly aimed at the 'end user' and not at a data processing department which might have come to an accommodation with 'computer American'.

If I hear you muttering 'what is there in all this for us', then one thing I would suggest is this. There are many IT and communications companies in considerable need of a 'language in the product' policy set by professionals who can also provide a service to implement it for them. Just as we specialise our marketing and products for the industry of our customers, so that we can make their application of IT a competitive advantage to them in their business, translators and interpreters can consider specialising in the rapidly growing, changing and converging industries of information technology and communications to our competitive advantage and your professional benefit.

And now to 1992 and all that. Our perception of what 'Europe *sans frontières*' means to European industry is as follows. Let us be quite clear about 1992 – it will happen, the internal barriers to trade will dramatically diminish – but desirable as that is, it is not the main benefit of '1992'. The most important payoff is for European companies to become strong enough to compete with, and beat, those of the other great technological and trading entities, currently the United States and Japan. This increased strength will come from access to and operation in a world-player size home market. Clearly, growing strong in this greatly enlarged home market will in itself involve intense competition between European companies with benefits to the consumer. But this is secondary to the ultimate aim. Indeed, this competition will also lead to synergy between companies. In the IT industry hardly anyone can expect to be the sole supplier to the larger users, themselves multinationals. So cooperation has to be part of the strategy of European IT companies. Therefore, we have to get better at communicating with each other in clear language so as to avoid unnecessary and expensive confusion, and we must look to your profession to help us in achieving this.

In this matter of how European companies can gain strength let us look at an example of what has been and what might be. I will take an example from telecommunications, as a change from IT. In most Member States of the European Community the telecommunications monopoly has also acted as the patron of so-called 'national champions'. It is the existence of these relationships between the PTT and the 'national champions' which resulted in European companies producing a plethora of equipment tailored to the specific needs, indeed the whims, of the PTTs. A recent report on telecommunications pointed out that the European companies had produced eleven different and competing types of digital switching equipment, whereas North American companies had produced only four for the whole North American market. How therefore are European companies ever likely to enjoy economies of scale on a par with their North American and Japanese competitors when they are denied access to their neighbours' markets in Europe? Exclusion of external competition has led to gross inefficiencies, wasted resources and higher costs to the consumer. Let us not forget the consumer. After all, we are all consumers!

Let me describe how the approach of 1992 is affecting the actions of STC and ICL. ICL has had an active presence across Europe for many years. We operate in every Member State of the EC and in most of the countries of the European Free Trade Association. We have now clearly stated to ourselves and publicly that our domestic market is the total European market of some 350 million people.

The STC Group of Companies are technology-based but market-driven. We operate at the 'leading edge' of communication and information systems. Our understanding of technology, and our awareness of the threat to our ambitions to grow our share of the total European market has convinced us that we need to become much more effective as a European player. It will come as no surprise to you that we began by cooperating with other European partners on pre-competitive research and development. We are already a major contributor to the UK's technology base. In 1987 the STC Group spent over £175 million of its own money on R&D – that represents something like 20 per cent of the total UK non-government-funded R&D in electronics.

STC is a member of the European Community Round Table which was established by Viscount Davignon when he was a member of the Commission of the European Communities in order to develop a positive dialogue with European Community industrialists and a common European strategy for the high-technology industries. Between them, the twelve major European companies involved in the Round Table represent the bulk of the European high-technology electronic industries. These companies, including STC, are the major players in the Community's R&D framework programme. For STC the three most significant elements of the Framework Programme are the BRITE, RACE and ESPRIT efforts, particularly ESPRIT which focuses on IT R&D. STC is a member of the ESPRIT Steering Committee and is directly involved in 35 ESPRIT projects, to which we have committed some 500 man-years of technical and scientific resource. However, before ESPRIT and the other Community programmes took off, ICL, with Bull and Siemens, had already established the privately-funded European Centre for Computer Research in Munich. This centre is now internationally recognised as one of the leading centres for research into areas of fifth generation computer technology.

ICL has played a leading role in the development of Open Systems Interconnection (OSI) in Europe. OSI will ultimately permit information systems to communicate with each other, which will enable users to 'mix and match' equipment from competing vendors. Notice the emphasis on improving communication – even if it is by machine.

In anticipation of the single market, in 1985 the Chairman of ICL established a high-level panel to formulate policies to ensure that ICL prospers from the creation of 'Europe without frontiers'. Recently, that panel has been transformed into a European Strategy Board to coordinate the company's operations throughout Europe and, in particular, to ensure that our management in the United Kingdom and in Continental Europe can utilise our total resources in the most effective manner to exploit our strengths in our chosen specialisations. The President of ICL Europe and the Managing Director of ICL UK Ltd, assisted by this Board, are charged with making Europe our home market and completing the transformation of a British company, with 'Old Commonwealth' and Continental connections, into a European Multinational.

I hope that I have shown you how we are preparing ourselves for the challenges and opportunities of Europe in the 1990s. But although we in ICL are pushing for the swift elimination of national barriers to trade within Europe, no-one believes that the cultural barriers, often based on language, will go. Indeed, it would be a sad and unwelcome day for Europe if 'Europe without frontiers' resulted in a homogenisation of our cultural differences and, with it, our intellectual vigour. Greater communication between Europeans, and between Europe and the rest of the world, should be encouraged and enabled by better and more sophisticated communications and information systems. After all, we in the STC Group want to stay in business! But, ultimately, people will still need to communicate ideas, plans and dreams. This will still be done person to person and that is your expertise.

Perhaps we might allow ourselves a verse to sum up what 'Europe *sans frontières*' is to help us to avoid.

> Our choicest dreams have fallen through
> Our airiest castles tumbled down
> Because of lines we neatly drew
> And later neatly tumbled over.

So, the industry with which I am familiar suggests two major areas where 1992 will drive us into your arms. One is that language will become embedded in the product to a crucial degree, and this will inevitably lead to demand for your services as an intimate part of our design processes. The second is that within multinationals like ourselves, and between collaborating business partners, there will be a key need for accurate and clear person to person communication, both by word of mouth and by document.

I am sure that there are many other examples to be drawn from other firms and other industries. But since, fundamentally, business is about business and competition, I will conclude with a plug. As it says in the ICL advertisements – 'We should be talking to each other'.

Session 1: Multilingual marketing

Chaired by Norman Boakes

Multilingual business-to-business marketing

Alan J. Gilderson

Copy Director, Business-to-Business Information i Helsingborg AB, Helsingborg, Sweden

This paper deals with the special linguistic needs of companies that market products and services to professional buyers in export markets.

The internationalisation of business and the high cost of house-call selling have made central production of advertising, marketing and technical literature the most cost-effective way to communicate with target groups which are small in numbers, but geographically and linguistically widespread.

Multilingual business-to-business information makes special demands that affect all phases of production: text, artwork, layout, mechanical reproduction, and last but not least translation.

There is a growing need for a new breed of marketing-oriented translator capable of treating the source text as a copy platform for creative adaptation to inform and persuade professional buyers in a language they recognise and accept as their own.

INTRODUCTION

My subject is multilingual business-to-business marketing. To put it in its proper perspective I shall have to take it in reverse order: first what I mean by marketing, then how business-to-business marketing differs from consumer marketing, and finally why the language aspect is so very important and what it takes to produce good translations of business-to-business marketing material.

Let us start with some definitions.

Marketing is another of those words like love and democracy that cause an awful lot of confusion because they mean different things to different people. So to make sure that we understand each other, I'll give you the one that my colleagues and I work by:

Marketing is the commercial process of identifying and satisfying needs.

We could spend hours discussing the implications of that, but I've only got half an hour, so I'll have to ask you to take it on trust. The main point I want to make with it is that marketing is not just a fancy word for selling. Selling is just a part of a very complex process that can only work properly with a two-way flow of information between buyer and seller. If the seller knows exactly what the buyer wants and the buyer knows exactly what the seller is offering, they can do business with a fair chance that both will come away satisfied and be willing to do business with each other again.

Business-to-business marketing is the process of supplying goods and services not to private individuals for their personal use and enjoyment, but to buyers in industry, commerce and the public sector who use those goods and services directly or indirectly to produce other goods and services. I am not going to discuss international marketing of consumer goods. In the first place it's organised differently, in the second place it would take too long and in the third place I'm not qualified to talk about it. Even on the subject of business-to-business communication I shall have to confine myself to one aspect: advertising. Advertising is just one of the many phases of the marketing communication process, the one concerned with making first contact between buyer and seller. But it will do as an illustration.

THE TARGETS OF BUSINESS-TO-BUSINESS MARKETING

Marketing is a process of communication. Let's see whom we are trying to communicate with in business-to-business marketing. Our target groups are hard-nosed professional buyers whose buying decisions may make or break their companies. And they have two other characteristics that make them very different from the targets of consumer marketing:

1. *They are few.* If you're selling branded toiletries or groceries, you've got tens of millions of potential customers in the United Kingdom alone and possibly billions on the world market. But if you're selling machine tools, you're down to a few hundred thousand. And if your product is nuclear powered icebreakers, you can count your customers without taking your other hand out of your pocket.

2. *They are geographically widespread.* There is an old saw that all business is local, but nowadays you have to do local business in a lot of places, especially if your business is business-to-business. Indeed, you may not have enough domestic customers to support your business. One of my Swedish clients, for example, makes refractories for aluminium smelting plants. There is exactly *one* aluminium smelting plant in Sweden, but a few hundred scattered around the world. So business-to-business marketing is often international by necessity, and it looks like getting more so – not just in the upcoming European Inner Market, but all over the world. High-tech industry isn't the private preserve of Europeans and Americans any more.

So how do we make contact with our far-flung target group?

HOW BUSINESS-TO-BUSINESS ADVERTISING WORKS

It is a fact little known outside the trade that *industrial products are not sold: they are bought.* In business-to-business deals, it is nearly always the buyer who takes the initiative and searches actively for the product he needs. So there's no need to send salesmen to look for customers. That's very expensive if you reckon a typical cost of a couple of hundred pounds per sales call and a success rate of maybe 5 per cent. By advertising, you can make customers come to you. It's much cheaper and more efficient. By advertising in this context I do not mean television spots or colour spreads in glossy magazines. My agency produces a certain amount of trade press advertising, but only as a backup. The medium we use most is direct mail – brochures, catalogues, samples and other informative material sent direct to named persons in specified industries.

We are located in Sweden, where manufacturers have a small domestic market, so about 80 per cent of what we produce is aimed at export markets. Using the same material on different national markets is perfectly feasible, because industrial products are used for the same purposes and in the same ways everywhere. Central production of standard material saves a lot of money, and also gives the manufacturer better control over the message that goes out to buyers – much better than letting national sales companies do their own thing.

Standardisation, however, does not extend to language. You can get away with doing the whole thing in English if you're aiming at international top management, but I don't recommend it because you improve the odds of getting a response if you address people in their own language.

The sales brochures we produce for our clients are typically printed in about 10,000 copies. Half of those are in English and the rest divided between three or more other languages. First we make blanks, which are colour prints of all the illustrations without text. Then we overprint those with text in different languages, which can be done with one black and white film per language. The total production cost runs to something like £50,000, which means that each copy costs £5. But if just one copy brings in an enquiry that leads to a contract for a ship or an aeroplane or a building, it pays for the other 9,999. That is an extreme case, of course. In practice we have calculation models that can accurately predict the return on a given investment in marketing communication.

TECHNIQUES OF MULTILINGUAL PRODUCTION

There are rules for producing that kind of material that we have learned the hard way. The basic ones are:

1. *Account executives* must learn to include translation time in campaign schedules. The quality of translation varies inversely with the time allowed.

2. *Art directors* must learn to leave vacant space in the layout, and preferably group text and visuals in separate blocks. A translation is *always* longer than the original copy. And they must not use reversed text, except plain white on black. White on colour means you cannot use blanks.

3. *Copywriters* must be aware that what they write is going to be translated — and quite likely mistranslated if they do not make their meaning clear. Also, punning headlines are out, unless you give the translator an alternative version to work from.

THE INFORMATION COMPONENT

The text content of business-to-business advertising is very important. The more factual information you can feed the clients that way, the more easily they can judge whether they're really interested in what you have to offer, and the less expensive time salesmen have to spend making a pitch. Ideally, the client should be sufficiently interested and informed that a salesman is *sent* for because he or she is ready to buy.

Here's a very simple product — a wood screw. It has a very low value per unit, but a substantial value in quantity. Even such a low-tech piece of hardware as a wood screw has an information component. It has no value at all without the basic information that its function is to fasten two pieces of wood together and that you need a screwdriver to install it. Too obvious? Only because we civilised types all know what screws are for and how to drive them. An Amazonian Indian might lack that essential information.

The products involved in business-to-business marketing are often much bigger and more complicated, and their value to the user depends to a much higher degree on the information that comes with them.

That is why the copy aspect — and by extension the translation aspect — is so important.

TRANSLATION OF BUSINESS-TO-BUSINESS ADVERTISING COPY

And now we are finally down to the nitty-gritty of business-to-business translation. In my experience it calls for a special kind of translation ability that is rare — but I believe it can be cultivated.

I am now about to propound two heresies. I hope you will give me time to defend them before rushing me to the stake.

HERESY 1
Accurate translation is no good
to multinational business-to-business marketers.

My experience as a buyer of translations has been that translators have too much respect for the source text at the expense of the end result. At our agency we usually write the original copy in English and have it translated into other languages. One of the commonest complaints we get from our clients' European sales organisations is that the French, German or whatever sounds too much like English. I can illustrate the kind of thing I mean with a passage from a brochure that we had translated from Swedish into English. It was about computer control of central heating and air conditioning systems. I quote:

> *Komfort är idag detsamma som god ekonomi. Prestationen ökar hos dem som arbetar i fastigheten om klimat och miljö är bra. I restaurangen eller hotellet ökar trivseln hos gästerna och på ett sjukhus mår patienterna bättre. En god komfort får omedelbart angenäma konsekvenser för ekonomin, vilken miljö än handlar om.*
>
> Today, comfort is the same as good economy. Personal performance increases in a property where the climate and environment are good. Restaurants and hotels increase the pleasure of their guests, and patients in a hospital feel better. Good comfort has positive economical effects directly, whatever the environment or situation.

That was a perfectly correct translation from the Swedish. But if we'd printed the brochure in that kind of English, would you have bought the system on the strength of it? We had it done over by a copywriter, like this:

> Comfort is not a luxury: it makes sound economic sense. People work more efficiently in buildings with a comfortable indoor climate. Hotel guests sleep better. Restaurant guests enjoy their food more. Hospital patients feel better. It always pays to have alert employees and satisfied customers.

It would be nice if we could get that done in one operation by one person – straight from good advertising copy in language A to good advertising copy in language B.

It seems to me that a lot of translators are still hung up on a schoolchild attitude to their work: the need to prove to the teacher that they have understood everything in the original by reproducing it as faithfully as they can. But the readers of business-to-business marketing messages couldn't care less what the original said: what they want is information relevant to them in their own language.

So my first heresy is not so heretical after all. I am not advocating a reduction in standards of translation, but a more advanced form of translation.

I have written an instruction sheet that I enclose with all the translation orders I send out. The first and most important instruction reads:

> The person you are translating for is neither the writer of the original text nor the client who commissioned the writing of it, but the READER, i.e. the intended recipient of the client's message.

HERESY 2
A business-to-business translator
does not have to be a subject specialist.

A business-to-business advertising copywriter is expected to be able to write about *anything*. In my time I have written about dairying, offshore oil rigs, dental alloys, acoustics, freezers, furnaces and sewage treatment, none of which I knew a thing about to begin with. All it takes is time, research and close collaboration with the client.

So why should a translator not be able to do likewise – given time, research and close collaboration with the client?

My defence of this heresy is much the same as for the first one. The added value that a translator can contribute to the business-to-business communication process lies not in a knowledge of terminology or specialists' jargon, but in being able to write well and persuasively in a language that potential buyers accept because they recognise it as their own.

INTERACTIVE TRANSLATION

You may think some of my remarks have been unduly hard on translators. But buyers of translations are often at fault too. The practice of sending texts away for translation with no covering message except a required delivery date – usually much too close – is an insult to the profession, and needs to be stamped out.

As a translator, I get very annoyed if somebody expects me to translate a picture caption without sight of the picture. As a buyer of translations, I try to practise what I preach and give my translators the fullest possible briefing.

I don't think business-to-business marketers will get better translations of their marketing messages unless they get much closer to their translators. But that also means the translators must be prepared to come and meet them half-way.

Translators have got to come down out of their ivory towers and stop being anonymous. And clients have got to welcome their translators aboard as members of the creative team. Not necessarily on payroll, but as professional consultants.

To do a good job, translators need all the information they can get. They can't get it all through a Post Office or electronic mailbox. Clients should invite their translators to the factory to see and handle the products they are expected to write about, and there should be direct dialogue between everybody involved.

That, by the way, includes the client's national sales companies and agents. It's a matter of psychology. If a UK exporter sends out ready-translated brochure material in French, German and Italian, the local people are apt to criticise the language, shove it on a back shelf and not use it. But if they are consulted during its preparation, they will accept it. The translator has to be involved in that process.

It is a process of give and take. The translator should not accept the original text uncritically. If he thinks it needs adapting for readers in the target country, he should say so and explain why. By doing so he is serving the best interests of his client.

CONCLUSION

To sum up, then, manufacturing companies and advertising agencies who produce multinational business-to-business information need access to translators who are able and willing to come out of the woodwork and be active, interactive members of the team.

This kind of collaboration demands a lot more time and work than straight translation, but – and here comes the sugar on the pill – it motivates an entirely different scale of fees.

By no means all the companies or agencies who need that kind of translation service know that they need it. As long as they don't know it, as long as they continue to accept 'accurate' translations, they will lose out to competitors who have realised that translation, too, must be good advertising copy.

Business-to-business marketing presents both a challenge and an opportunity to the translating profession. The challenge is to develop the special skills needed, and to educate users to take advantage of those skills. If we succeed, we will have broken into a growth sector that will make the profession of translating much more profitable, and much more fun too.

Interpreting and the international outlook

Valerie Landon

Freelance interpreter

> With 1992 in mind, and all its implications so far as selling in a multi-lingual market is concerned, industry should be carefully considering its attitude to linguists.
>
> Companies may choose not to use interpreters for many reasons, not the least being the expense involved, fears about finding someone with the necessary expertise and the feeling that a member of the firm with some knowledge of the language needed can probably do the job perfectly well. However, to participate fully in the international scene, particularly from 1992 onwards, it must be realised that many influential and educated potential clients or business associates do not necessarily speak sufficient English to conduct transactions in that language. Having found the right interpreter (not always as easy as it sounds), it will almost certainly mean that business relations will be greatly improved and British companies will be able to compete on equal terms with their European counterparts.

I am going to speak on 'interpreting and the international outlook', but I do not intend to speak of today, rather of the future. Not the very distant future, however, but of 1992. This is the date when we become part of a truly common market. From snippets appearing increasingly in the newspapers we learn that hopefully the creation of a unified European market by 1992 will save the EEC up to £175 billion and add 5 per cent to Europe's growth rate. These figures are given by the European Commission. The single market should lead to a regeneration of European commerce, through economies of scale, as companies operate on a Europe-wide basis, and through job creation, healthier competition, stable prices and business and professional mobility. Consumer prices should fall, as should unemployment, etc. However, I shall not be discussing these aspects of 1992, nor of such problems as a common policy for VAT. What interests me is the question of unity and strength. The intention is that a real common market will allow European countries to compete on equal terms with the mega-economies of Japan and the United States and, by generating increased internal trade, jerk the West European economy out of its 1980s lethargy.

The French, as part of their 1992 press and TV campaigns (of which more later) have been showing a television advertisement in which a feeble French businessman, in his shorts, squares up to a formidable Japanese sumo wrestler and a grizzly American baseball player. Unable to beat them on his own, he enlists the aid of eleven other sportsmen, wearing the colours of each EC Member State. The combination of all twelve European nations then proves too much for either the Japanese or the American. The moral is: unification in 1992 is essential for victory against the industrial giants. Which leads me naturally to a much older tale of unification and strength: that of the Tower of Babel. In the book of Genesis the Lord says: 'Behold they are one people, and they have all one language and this is only the beginning of what they will do', and it goes on: 'so he confused their languages and scattered them abroad'. In the same way, one of the strengths of the Church in mediaeval times was the fact that it had a unifying language, Latin, that was written and spoken by all educated men (and women?). From this we may therefore conclude that one of the necessary things, in order to achieve unity and successful attainment of a common goal, is the possibility of a common language. As was recently written with regard to the importance of 1992 to British business: 'Only the small residual problem of differing languages will hinder this new Europe from becoming as powerful an economic engine as the United States and Japan'. I am not sure if this was meant to be ironic, but I am sure all the linguists here will clearly see the irony of it.

Is this perhaps the moment for Esperanto to take its place as a universal language, to be taught as a compulsory second language in all schools of those countries hoping to be part of the 1992 Common Market? (or Latin. . .?). I must at this point admit to a rather special affection for Esperanto, as I once lived in the house where Dr Zamenhof was born. But of course this is not what I have in mind, because were Esperanto to fulfil this role it would already have experienced far more success in the 101 years since its creation. And as for Latin – the state of classical education in the secondary schools of Europe does not suggest a breakthrough on this front either. What of course is more likely to happen is that probably one or two languages will become a predominant group, and it is these languages that will eventually become the lingua franca of the European Common Market. Will English be part of this grouping? That is something to which I shall return at the end of this paper.

So, what I am really postulating is that everyone, whatever his or her career, be he or she scientist or engineer, lawyer or doctor, ticket collector or shop assistant, must learn at least one language other than his or her own, and preferably two. And it is of course here that we lag so lamentably behind our European neighbours (and competitors). Rare is the French engineer who does not speak English, rarer still is the Dutch one who does not speak English and French or German, and fluently, at least in his or her own discipline. Recently on the radio I heard a representative of the French seamen (a member of the CGT) talking in fluent English about the P&O ferry strike. Buy a ticket in a German station – the man behind the counter is perfectly capable of answering your questions in English. Just imagine the situation reversed in England.

But of course from the interpreter's point of view, or rather from the point of view of the interpreter in industry, it means that since the ideal situation of only one common language does not exist, and is not likely to (due perhaps to the same national pride that prevented the harmonisation of all sausages of the twelve nations into one Eurosausage in 'Yes Minister'), and since the second best situation, that of multilingualism, is still a long way off in the future, our role in business can only grow and grow.

But industry must be aware of what is happening and be prepared to face up to the challenge of the other eleven countries. To come back to what is happening in France as only one example, the French have seized the lead in their rush to become more European. It would even seem, according to one Sunday paper, that the 'risks and opportunities of 1992 have virtually replaced sex, food and the property market as topics of conversation', and the Government has been running 1992 press and television campaigns for the past eighteen months. We must be absolutely sure that we are not left behind – apparently research campaigns conducted in the last year have shown that reactions from business people tend to be that they 'have never heard of it, it will probably never happen anyway because no one will agree to it and even if it does happen it will never affect me'. A bit like the general attitude to Aids. The CBI even claims that firms that do not prepare risk being rapidly forced out of business – this may be said to shock but there is no reason to believe that it is not true.

So, eventually, what does it all mean? It means that hopefully businesses will be able to sell their products in wider markets than they ever imagined, and not only will these goods have to be technically acceptable to comply with regulations in other states, but all aspects of marketing them will have to conform or be acceptable to the prospective buyers. And this has to be where the role of the linguist comes into its own.

We are all familiar with ghastly translations of handbooks and instruction manuals. This assumes that we have even bought the product. But the charm of a certain French soft drink called 'Pschitt' may be lost on the Anglo-Saxon purchaser, as may that of an aperitif from further afield (Japan) that bears the delightful name of 'Swet'; and does the name 'Athlete's Foot' really entice you when you are shopping for footwear? Logically, therefore, industry should be using us. Not just interpreters, although never being over-modest we realise just how important we are, but also translators and multilingual media people for advertising, promotion, etc., of their products. Because we are not just language experts, we also understand (or should), and are familiar with, the culture and customs of the country or countries whose language we speak. We are thus in a unique position to give advice about how to target the consumer and what approach to take.

There are a great many reasons why industry does not use us, and I am going to discuss some of them – businessmen would no doubt be able to think of many more – and attempt to convince them that they are wrong and should be thinking of us being as much a part of their team as designers, managers, salesmen, etc. I cannot decide whether the biggest single reason why we are not used is the expense or that people do not really know where to look for us.

Let us start with the question of cost. Obviously when you use an interpreter it can be fairly costly and there is no apparent direct return. But it is essential that companies start to think of us in a different way. We are professionals as are accountants, solicitors and stockbrokers. And we probably come a lot less expensive. There are few accountants who charge less than £35 per hour. I know of many who charge £100 plus, as do many solicitors. I do not think there are many interpreters (taking an average of the above-mentioned prices) who charge £400 to £500 per day. Of course, an accountant saves a business money (or should), and so might we if misunderstandings are avoided and time saved, or we might even make it, i.e. money, if orders are placed with our help. Of all countries, Great Britain should understand about the value of service industries – they (e.g. insurance, banking, etc.) are one of our major strengths – and that is how interpreting should be considered. We are professionals, practising a profession. How many times have I been told by a businessman, when I have been accompanying a Government delegation from abroad: 'You won't have too much to do today – my secretary speaks French'. I was even told once, at an official dinner, by a businessman who had just told a poor joke 'I'm glad my secretary will be there tomorrow' (when we were due to visit his factory), 'she'll be able to translate my jokes much better than you'. And how often have I had to step into the breach, when the poor girl has found that her 'O' or even 'A' level French was not adequate to explain the intricacies of a complicated engineering process that I had spent most of the previous two or three days mugging up, both linguistically and technically, so that I could 'perform' in an intelligent and intelligible way.

The next problem for the person in business is finding us. People often take my card when I am on assignment and tell me that they really could use someone like me, now that they know where to find me. What does one do when one needs an interpreter? Do you telephone an agency picked from the *Yellow Pages*, or ask if the sales manager has any relations who speak French, or resort to the filing clerk, who spent last summer camping in Normandy? Obviously, the first solution has to be a good one, but perhaps better still approach a professional body (particularly now that one exists). This might of course have presented problems in the past. That has to be the first step, but the company must explain its requirements clearly in order that the best person can be found for the job. They must specify, first and foremost, what language combinations are required (this is not as self-evident as it sounds). As an aside here I must say that when I read the advertisements in the papers I am always astonished when I read an advertisement for a linguist (usually for some kind of office job), where, for example, a fluent French speaker is required; or Spanish would do – is it assumed that if one can speak one language one will automatically be able to speak another? The company must also specify what the subject-matter is likely to be (we are not all automatically experts in every subject); they must say what type of interpreting is required. Is it to be a 'real' conference (interpreters in booths); is it to be round table discussions where everything will have to be translated consecutively from one language to another; is it to be a discussion, relatively formal or informal; is it to accompany someone on the tour of a factory? If and when all these things are known, it is much easier to recommend the right person. Now that we have a professional body that groups us together, this part of the task should be much easier; and of course there are always reputable agencies, that have in the past catered adequately and efficiently for business's needs if they have wished to use them, and no doubt will continue to do so.

Perhaps a company is concerned about using us because we are not really part of that company – are they at risk as far as their industrial and professional secrets are concerned? I think that this is a real fear, and one that is not often voiced. After all, we work for many companies, bodies, organisations, how can one be sure of our discretion? This is, I admit, an extremely tricky problem, and one on which it is impossible to give guarantees for anyone other than oneself. But I must reiterate that we are professional people, that we have our code of ethics, and an indiscreet interpreter would not, I imagine, have very much work for long. We are trying to present ourselves to you with a professional image, and part of that involves mutual trust.

A final reason that I can think of for a firm not wishing to use interpreters is that we have a reputation, very often, for being difficult and temperamental, as well as costly. This is something on which perhaps it would be tactful for me not to comment too deeply, but I think that on the whole if you treat us well, we will try to do our very best. My own feeling is that I have done my job really well when I have been invisible – when no-one thanks me at the end of a meeting I always like to assume that it is because I have been so efficient that it has not been noticed that I was there – that what I said was so accurate, and so in the spirit of the original that people felt they were speaking directly to each other 'eyeball to eyeball', and not via an intermediary. We can certainly fulfil this role much better if the client has gone to the trouble to brief us adequately, has let us see relevant documents (preferably bi- or multilingual ones) in advance of the meeting, perhaps has even met us, or at least spoken to us on the telephone to tell us a little of what is likely to happen. I think part of our reputation for being temperamental arises from the fact that we tend to not want to work more than seven or eight hours at a stretch. In fact, this is to protect the clients as well as us – there is a limit to our concentration and after a very long period we do not always give of our best, which helps neither them nor us.

Having, I hope, demolished some of the arguments against the use of interpreters, I should now like to return to 1992 and all that. Recently, Lord Young visited Japan and on his return he emphasised the need for exporters to use Japanese when seeking to sell there. So far afield. . . . First of all let us look much closer to home – surely it is just as important to use the languages of Europe when seeking to sell in a single European market? What is being attempted by the European Commission, in the words of Lord Cockfield, its vice-president, is 'a community in which traders could do business with customers in other member states, just as they do with customers in the next street or the next town'. The time has really come to stop thinking that everyone speaks English, or if they do not they ought to; and that they will understand somehow, even if not adequately or correctly.

It must be realised that many influential and educated potential clients or business associates do no necessarily speak sufficient English to conduct transactions in that language. And here we must look further than Europe, to Japan for example, as Lord Young says, or to the Arab states. No self-respecting Japanese company would send someone to Great Britain to do business unless he spoke the language or was accompanied by an interpreter who did. The Department of Trade and Industry has already launched its campaign to make industry and commerce more aware of the implications of the single market. Lord Young, in his launch speech, said that harmonisation in Europe will involve choosing priorities. According to him, and in line with my ideas of course, the Government does not see high on its list either taxation, such as value added tax, or Britain joining the European Monetary System. A common European currency seems to present the same problems as a common language. In fact, Lord Young said: 'It does not matter whether we all have the same rates of VAT or tax. The priority is having similar products, like an electric plug that can be used in any of the European countries'. Alan Sugar, Chairman of Amstrad, clearly agreed with this when he said: 'Thanks to bureaucracy I have to make a different computer for every EEC country. By the end of 1992 everything will be different. . .'. Lord Young then went on to say that the United States was a single market, but every state had its own taxes. Which brings me back to one of my original points, and one which (at least in the report of the speech that I read), Lord Young seems to have failed to make. The United States has its own federal system, its separate methods of taxation in each state, but it has one common language, and therein lies its strength. The Department of Trade and Industry has chosen such well-known people as Bruce Oldfield, the dress designer, Alan Sugar, the Amstrad chairman, Richard Rogers, the architect and Sir John Egan, the chairman of Jaguar, to be joined later by Richard Branson, the Virgin boss, Lord Forte, chairman of the Trust House Forte hotel and catering group, and Mary Quant, also a designer, to help boost its three month television campaign. These people have been chosen because they have already been successful in Europe. However, it must be remembered that the British are notoriously an insular people ('Fog over the Channel − Continent cut off' as they said in the nineteenth century), and for most of them, the belief that foreigners begin at Calais may stay unchanged despite the breaking down of Europe's barriers. The test for all companies will be to start thinking in European terms. In future the domestic market for British goods and services will not stop at Dover but will cover an 884,000 square mile area, extending to Jutland and the Peloponnese, from Salonika to Stornaway. So what has not been said? Exactly what I have said before. Oldfield admits that during his early exporting days it was all a bit difficult, i.e. form filling was a nightmare, customs, transfers and the whole business of getting the product to the client was difficult. I do not know if Oldfield (or indeed any of the others mentioned above) is a linguist, but if and when industry can be persuaded that English is not a universal language (at least in Europe), whatever it may be in the United States; when it can be made to understand that part of the cost of investing in its future should include the use of properly trained linguists for all aspects of its work, I think a great step forward will have been achieved. What is the good of a beautiful glossy brochure, costing a lot of money, if it is incomprehensible to a large percentage of the potential customers?

Hopefully, at least for industry, using interpreters will only represent an interim step. That will be the case if either everyone involved in multinational activities becomes fluent in one of the group of languages that will become those of habitual use in the European Common Market, or learns Esperanto. Will English be one of these? It should be stated here that English is an international rather than a European language. The CBI feels that the transformation of the market in less than five years time should be a central concern of chief executives. And one of their main preoccupations should be the question of how they will cope linguistically with the challenge. If they want to be first in the market place when 'Europe' is 'Open for Business' (the slogan for the Government campaign), industry must start now to use interpreters (and all other linguists), so that when the time comes, we, as well as they, are properly prepared, properly able to work together, understanding each other's roles. We are much more likely to arrive at true unity if we can communicate without difficulty, and communication can only mean language.

Let us hope that the situation at the end of last October, when a Department of Trade and Industry survey showed that only 15 per cent of businessmen even knew significant changes were in the offing (as opposed to 80 per cent in France) will rapidly change, so that the target of 90 per cent awareness is reached for the end of this year. And hopefully this awareness will include also an understanding of the needs I have already enumerated with regard to the activities of companies in a multinational setting.

Let us not make the kind of error that can occur when someone with a limited knowledge of another language decides to dispense with the services of an interpreter. Thus did a businessman from overseas, who visiting the British subsidiary of his company for the first time, and wishing to rally his new all-British team, exhorted them to follow the example of members of the company in his own country who, in order to vanquish the competition, made it a regular habit to 'be early to bed and up with the cock'.

Well, we must be ready too, and in order to beat the competition, let us also be early to bed but – early to rise!

The multilingual manufacturer

John Seager

Duracell plc

Note from the Editor:
I am sorry to have to tell readers that this paper has not been supplied to us in written form. I reproduce below a copy of the abstract supplied by Mr. Seager in advance of the conference. In addition, Mr. Seager amplified some of the points he made in his talk during the discussion session.

An examination, based upon nearly thirty years practical experience, of the factors influencing multilingual usage in the manufacturing industry with particular reference to multinationals.

The component functions of the manufacturing industry will be analysed to identify the natural tendency of different functions towards monolingualism. This will be followed by a discussion of the ways in which widening supply frontiers, expanding technical influence, relationships with company marketing units and, above all, the nature and degree of influence exerted by the parent company will influence the natural tendencies.

In conclusion, a brief examination will be made of the opportunities which exist within the manufacturing industry for the use of interpretation and translation skills and how these opportunities can best be developed.

Session 1: Report of discussion

Rapporteur: Melanie Dean, Rhône-Poulenc Ltd

The session chairman, Norman Boakes of Euro Marketors Partnership Ltd, asked each speaker to comment briefly on what he or she considered to be the role of languages in industry. Alan Gilderson emphasised the importance of incorporating linguistic skills within the framework of any large organisation and of providing target-orientated translations. Valerie Landon stressed the importance of convincing industry of the need to use the services of the well-informed interpreter, and said that, in many cases, interpreters undervalued their own services. John Seager, drawing on his own experience, explained that many multinational organisations did not require the services of freelance interpreters and translators as such skills could often be found in-house.

The floor was then opened to questions and comments.

In response to Valerie Landon's paper, Jamila Bernat from Just Words (Arabic), London, said that interpreters did not undervalue their own services although their clients tended to do so. She explained how, in her experience, solicitors often considered interpreters' fees to be excessive, and that court interpreters were sometimes expected to attend hearings without having had access to the relevant documentation. In her reply, Valerie Landon referred to the main theme of her paper, 'unity is strength', emphasising that interpreters should refuse to appear in court unless they received adequate support and confirmation of payment from their clients. John Seager said that interpreting called for high professional standards and should be remunerated accordingly. William Masen of Interlingua TTI Ltd pointed out that interpreters should be paid agreed rates and not legal aid rates. Fees should be quoted clearly in writing and then clients would be obliged to pay.

Eyvor Fogarty, freelance translator, asked Alan Gilderson whether his company collaborated with advertising agencies under formal arrangements and whether he provided guidelines for translators when commissioning work. In reply, Alan Gilderson explained that his company collaborated with agencies in most European countries on the basis that if, for example, publicity material was required in German, he would contact the advertising agency in Germany which, by prior agreement, would provide the necessary information. With regard to guidelines, translators would be provided with any relevant documentation and sales material; they would also have access to the client and to his or her representative in their home country.

Commenting on Alan Gilderson's view that translations should be target-orientated as opposed to source-orientated, Bruno Berger, freelance translator from Germany, concurred with his observation and stipulated that the same length of time should be allocated for the translation of a text as for the writing of the original.

Gordon Stuart, freelance translator, commented on how refreshing it was to hear of Duracell's multilingual approach, but was this very typical? John Seager explained that Duracell's approach was unusual in so far as several of its Marketing Directors were linguists and that the Company had developed its own technical language. He added that these factors largely contributed to Duracell's success in international markets.

Barbara Snell, freelance translator, wondered whether we confused potential clients by emphasising the distinction between translators and interpreters. Would it not be more appropriate to use the term 'linguist' instead? This comment received a mixed response from the audience. Valerie Landon agreed that a translator with an extensive knowledge of a given subject should also be able to interpret in that field. She added that an 'overall linguist' would be extremely beneficial to most companies. John Seager thought that proficient interpreters probably could become good translators, but that the reverse was not necessarily the case. He considered that interpreting called for qualities in addition to linguistic ability. Pamela Mayorcas stated that, although translating and interpreting were related skills, they were not always happily combined.

It is interesting to note that, when this question was put to the audience, only six people agreed with the concept of the 'overall linguist'.

Aziza Molyneux-Berry, freelance interpreter, asked Valerie Landon what she considered would be the role of Arabic when trade within the EC became easier in 1992. Valerie Landon answered that, although she had referred mainly to the European languages in her paper, it was essential that all languages should be recognised. It should not be assumed that everyone spoke English.

Addressing his comments to John Seager, Kenneth Evans, a former staff translator now working freelance, said that, nowadays, there was a tendency in Germany and Switzerland to reduce in-house translation services. On the subject of fees, Mr Evans had also been told that his rates were excessive and that good translations could be obtained much more cheaply. However, this raised the fundamental question, who judges the quality of a translation, and what criteria are used to do so? Ulla Magnusson Murray, translation management consultant, agreed with Kenneth Evans that quality was of prime importance. She added that, as very few clients actually understood the language of the source text, they were not in a position to judge the quality of the translation. She suggested that, in order to overcome this problem, higher standards of foreign language teaching should be implemented in schools.

Sally Walker of Sally Walker Language Services, Bristol, thanked the speakers and Alan Gilderson in particular, as his paper related directly to her business. She explained that her approach was to educate clients to what they needed rather than to what they wanted. Directing further comments to John Seager and Michael Forrest, Sally Walker felt that, although their companies were impressive with regard to product development, especially language software, neither company had a specific policy regarding translation. This was essential as high quality, high speed and low cost could not be achieved at one and the same time.

Finally, Mary Cotton asked Alan Gilderson how best to approach the translation of a badly written original text. Alan Gilderson said that this was unfortunately a recurring problem; he, personally, adopted a policy of audience-specific translation and his clients now accepted the fact that their texts would not be translated literally. In conclusion, he suggested that, if the source text was of inferior quality, the author should be asked to rewrite it or else the translator should refuse to undertake the task.

After-lunch speech: Translators and interpreters mean business

John D. Graham

Mannesmann Demag, Duisburg, West Germany

It was with great pleasure that I accepted the unexpected invitation – or was it a challenge or even a dare? – from Peter Barber to make this 'impromptu' speech several months ago. He also gave me absolutely explicit instructions as to what not to say. What he didn't tell me was what to say. Consequently, after months of preparation intentions, I now have to present this more or less as an off-the-cuff examination of the title of this year's conference.

Had I liaised with our President, Professor Sager, or with any of the other guest speakers in the opening session, I would have known immediately what was meant by the title of the conference. As it was, I proceeded in textbook manner using my dictionary to find the appropriate meaning of the words themselves, always bearing in mind the definition of the translator as being someone, who, confronted with five possible meanings, chooses the sixth.

My dictionary – which I dare not mention in the presence of our most respected Chairman – shows me that 'business' can mean:

1. a money-making organisation or institution. The word 'money-making' convinced me that this was a most unlikely word to use in connection with the activities of translators and interpreters. So, I carried on searching for a more appropriate meaning.
2. an affair. Unlikely to be the meaning here.
3. an event, matter. Highly improbable.
4. an occupation or work. Getting warm. Could be right.
5. a trade. This last suggestion seemed to me to be the most likely, so I accepted it.

There has been a lot of talk by many people on many occasions as to what word best describes the métier of the translator or interpreter. One school would prefer the term 'the science of translation'. Another school refers to translation and interpreting as an art. There are those who suggest the word 'skill', which we would all accept as being at least conceptually correct but I prefer Professor Peter Newmark's term 'craft'. When a 'craft' is the means by which a livelihood is earned, the word 'trade' is as good a description as any other, i.e. 'the interpreting and translating trade'. Interestingly enough, by the way, what 'business' does not mean is busy-ness in the sense of assiduity, diligence or industry.

'Business' was, therefore, no real problem. However, I have to admit to a certain difficulty in the reading of the word 'mean' in the title. Is 'mean' an adjective? It certainly looks like it. It also makes sense.

The dictionary synonyms for 'mean' are:

1. inconsiderable.
2. selfish, small-minded, miserly. Sounds more like the people who hire translators and interpreters than the translators and interpreters themselves.
3. inferior in quality. Do I hear someone suggest that that is the correct adjective for the efforts of some of our less qualified brethren?
4. poor. This could be the correct definition.

'Translators and interpreters – a mean business.' But then the dash is missing.

Or could it be that 'mean' is used here as a noun? In which case, the dictionary offers:

1. anything halfway between two extremes. Not bad for a definition of translation in many respects.
2. the average. Like most of the translations we see – from others, especially non-ITI-members.
3. in the meaning 'wealth' or 'resources' or 'method', used only in the plural form.

I really would never have guessed that the word 'mean' was to be understood as the verb of intention, determination, willpower and purpose. If this really is the intended meaning, it would suggest that the invisible and anonymous translators and interpreters of the past are now actually intending to do something serious and constructive, to stand up and be counted. A professional attitude to professional problems involving discussion between all involved on an equal footing. That was often the case for the old Translators' Guild. Is that perhaps the secret of ITI's rapid success? A serious group of professionals, dedicated to perfection, responsibility and the maintenance of very high professional standards? Can it be that we are now about to make the attempt to convince the doubting Thomases of this world that we actually are a force to be reckoned with, to be taken seriously? I'd like to think so because that is the reason why I joined and why I supported the new institute from the very beginning. Nor can I think of a better place to make such a declaration of intent than London. After all, there are more nations represented in the telephone books of London's boroughs than in the United Nations – or on the books of some translation companies and agencies. As a graduate of London University, I have a long history of many good connections with

London. London is one of the busiest junctions in Britain. Just try getting to other parts of the United Kingdom from abroad without passing through London! It is easier to play Monopoly without passing 'Go'. It is also at the heart of British culture – and I do mean 'British' rather than 'English'.

The British culture – if there is such a thing – is a strange conglomerate. It bears distinct traces of virtually every other culture on earth. And with such panache! 'Kebab and chips' is taken just as much for granted as 'semi-detacheds in suburbia' – true to Wandruschka's theory that everybody speaks several languages every day. Excluding all refugees, foreigners, immigrants and citizens of former colonies, etc., this 'united' kingdom of ours itself is made up of four nations, each with its own highly individual culture, dialects, vocabularies and language, and with its own highly distinctive national characteristics.

There is the old joke which says:

> The Scots, who keep the Sabbath, and anything else they can lay their hands on;
> The Welsh, who pray on their knees – and also prey on their neighbours;
> The Irish, who have no idea what they want or where they are going – but are prepared to fight to the death for it; and
> The English, who are so proud of being a self-made race that they thereby relieve the Almighty of a dreadful responsibility.

This is, nevertheless, the *United* Kingdom! 'United' being the key word. It is this *uniting* aspect which binds us together in this Institute. It is our main endeavour to *unite* peoples of different cultures through our services as a linguistic bridge, a *uniting* link. The many thousands of nationals of countries from every part of the world resident in Britain and, in particular, here in London have also played their part in internationalising this land and its attitudes.

There are very few languages in this world which have not donated the odd word here and there – willingly or unwillingly – to the English language. This has resulted in a vocabulary of enormous wealth and a highly intricate but poorly defined grammatical structure in which the exceptions to the rule as a rule outnumber the rule, often by a vast majority, and where only the true British 'native' – born and bred on this sceptered isle – can 'know' instinctively what word should be used and in what context. It is a marvellously conceived device for keeping foreigners in their place by making them obvious, even in the event that they should have learned the rules well.

There are few understanding Britons indeed who would not agree that they are glad that they did not have to learn English as a foreign language and I am one of the very first to congratulate with all my heart those non-British – or non-English-mother-tongue nationals in our midst, who have persevered so long with our language that we have come to accept them at least as equals, if not, in all humility, as superior beings. An accolade indeed, and one which was mistakenly accorded me some years ago here in London when a dear Italian lady complimented me on my excellent command of English. She thought that it was almost impossible to detect my 'foreign' accent.

English, on the other hand, is anything but logical at times. The uninitiated have to shake their heads in incomprehension when they discover that the Square Tower is round, the Circular Quay is rectangular, a boxing ring is square. Nor is English always English. It is a language with a great many highly different faces. As Jean Rostand so aptly said: *On peut s'entendre avec ceux qui ne parlent pas la même langue, mais non pas avec ceux pour qui les mêmes mots n'ont pas le même sens.* This is especially true of English in the context of words of one language used to express a specific idea but which are used in other languages to mean something entirely different.

The idea of a universal language is Utopian. There will always be other languages – and rightly so. We must merely be prepared to learn one or two of them, without any thought of priority or rank. English may very well be important for many non-English-speaking countries such as Korea or China, but is it relevant in Czechoslovakia or Hungary?

I am reminded at this point of an article in *La Vanguardia* some years ago. The new representative of a major Japanese company in Spain was being interviewed. The reporter complimented him on his command of Spanish. The Japanese manager replied that it was company policy to have a good command of the language of the country in which they worked. The reporter recalled that this manager had just arrived from France. Did that mean that he could also speak French? Yes. In that case, said the reporter, the manager as a Japanese had his own mother tongue, had studied in America and therefore spoke English, had also learned French and now Spanish to a very high degree of competence and was therefore obviously the right person to answer a question which had been troubling him for some time: Which language was the most important language for international commerce in the present day and age? The Japanese manager replied immediately: the language of the customer. There can be few members of our Institute who do not subscribe to this principle. If we really mean business, it is now up to us to convince our customers that this precept is still valid.

Bearing in mind that there are more people on earth who speak English as their mother tongue or language of habitual usage or as their first or second foreign language than any other language including Chinese, we as members of this British Institute are in an excellent position to make a vital contribution to the success or failure of this world's technical, scientific, commercial and industrial endeavours.

Frank Schuitemaker's question is worth considering in this context: *Vertalen is een vak. Slechts weinigen beheersen het. Maar waarom leidt in onze vrije markteconomie deze zeldzaamheidswaarde niet tot hemelhoge prijzen?* [Translation is a skill. Few are those who master it. In that case, why does this product of such a rare gift not result in astronomical prices for their services?] To this quotation I have to add another – also in Dutch – by H. van Krimpen: *Goede vertalingen zijn duur, slechte nog veel duurder.* [Good translations are expensive – but bad translations are even more expensive.]

Our Institute has done much to further the translator's and the interpreter's cause and, at the same time, bridge the intercultural gap between nations, thus improving international communications. In this age of electronics, translation is instant and is consumed within minutes. This calls for a high degree of professionalism amongst those in the profession, a great deal of responsibility on the part of the members and of the Institute to safeguard and ensure that certain standards are met and maintained. It also means that translators and interpreters really do have to show that they mean business. After all, actions do speak much louder than words.

Session 2: Technology

Chaired by Pamela Mayorcas

The Terminological Information System (TIS) of the Council of Ministers of the European Communities

Christopher Burdon

Staff Translator at the Council of Ministers, Brussels, Belgium

Description of the work of the Council Secretariat and justification for developing our own system to range from monetary compensatory amounts to *la maladie de Newcastle*. Languages: F–D–DK–E–ES– GR (Greek)–IRL–NL–P (Portuguese)–LAT (Latin).

Accurate representation of characters: compromises rejected. Classification of data on input. Paramount importance of user-friendly routines. Developing a database for staff without computer experience.

Adoption of a decentralised approach based on existing administrative structures: the 'multi-bilingual' solution. Successful liaison with the computer experts: need for self-education.

Treatment of existing manual records. Computerised glossary production as a by-product. Commercial hardware and software used. Future public access?

Your Institute has kindly invited me to talk about the Terminological Information System (TIS) of the Council of Ministers of the European Communities. The Council of Ministers' Secretariat services the meetings of all the Government Ministers and civil servants coming to Brussels to discuss European matters, whether it be for European Councils – the so-called European summits – meetings of the Council of Ministers or routine working party proceedings. Hence, we provide facilities for no less than twelve governments.

Our translation work includes telexes calling meetings, briefing documents, agendas, speeches to be given by ministers and formal minutes written up after meetings have been held, plus the usual administrative translations needed in a multinational, multilingual organisation.

Much of the vocabulary we translate is either highly technical or else very specific to our organisation and we attach considerable importance to getting our terminology right!

Britain was a latecomer to the Common Market and most of the structures and working practices of the Council of Ministers were already fixed when we joined. The pioneer translators of those days often had to translate difficult concepts of continental law and administrative practice under great pressure of time. This type of vocabulary has now become enshrined in the Institution and for the sake of legal consistency staff translators are obliged to follow the precedents.

The Translation Directorate of the General Secretariat is organised into nine translation divisions: French, German, Danish, English and Irish (since that Division covers both the English and Irish languages), Greek, Italian, Dutch, Spanish and Portuguese. Almost all Council documents are translated into all these languages, although only Treaties and similar documents are translated into Irish. Additionally, the database makes provision for Latin which is used for the scientific names of plants, fishes, etc.

ORGANISATION OF THE TERMINOLOGY SERVICE

The separate language divisions have tended to work as self-contained units developing their own terminology card files or, in the case of one or two divisions, publishing their own specialised bilingual glossaries [1]. One or two multilingual glossaries [2] have been published in certain specialised areas.

A few years ago it was realised that there were vast quantities of information in all the divisions which, if successfully integrated, would considerably improve the functioning of the terminologists within the divisions. These terminologists are volunteers and are coordinated by a Central Terminology Office which provides additional back-up services.

I was working as a volunteer part-time terminologist in the English Division when the initial discussions for computerising terminology took place. The original contract was awarded to the Belgian subsidiaries of the British company ICL and the Italian company Olivetti, with ICL providing the mainframe computer and Olivetti word processor terminals. Since this was a fixed price contract – a debatable decision in itself – the input of the future users into the design of the system had to be limited. The companies involved had to meet a delivery deadline and were obviously not willing to allow a significant cost overrun at their own expense.

Hence, they were unwilling to have users constantly changing their minds about what they required. Their attitude was strengthened by the fact that we were requesting changes on the basis of our theoretical needs without having had any practical experience of using computers. In retrospect, it does not seem surprising that the system delivered to us two years ago was barely usable. Judging from what one reads in the press, this is not an unusual state of affairs [3].

DESCRIPTION OF TIS

Well, what is so unique about this system? After all, the Commission's multilingual system, Eurodicautom, has existed for many years and has become an increasingly sophisticated tool. Why did the Council of Ministers want its own terminology computer when it had the Commission's mature and well-developed system available online in its offices? What we wanted was a sort of Eurodicautom plus.

Greek

From the outset it was vital for Greek to be treated as the equal of the other languages, without compromises being made. This meant that one should be able to ask the system questions in Greek, type commands in the Greek alphabet, have the Greek characters correctly displayed on the screen, have the correct keyboard for touch-typing in Greek, have a printer which would correctly print Greek characters and have data-sorting routines that would respect the alphabetical order of the Greek language. I might add that the same demands were made for Danish and for the other Community languages. I am happy to say that ICL, the main contractors, and Olivetti satisfied these requirements very early in the development stages.

Other languages

That was not all. We also required the specific characters of other languages to be treated correctly: umlauts in German, the characteristic Danish vowels, æ, ø and å in both lower and upper case, and their correct representation in the system index so that they were fully distinguishable from ae, o and a which they superficially resemble in the eyes of people unfamiliar with Danish. The Danes were adamant that, in searching for terms, there should be no confusion between words such as *so* (meaning 'sow' in English) and *sø* (meaning 'lake'). French accents presented less of a problem since in French dictionaries they are not significant for alphabetic order. However, correct printing and screen display were needed.

DISTRIBUTION OF TERMINALS

As originally envisaged, the system was going to be very small, with one terminal per language division. However, once the system's potential was grasped, it became clear that we should aim ultimately to give a terminal to any translator who requested one. We have not yet achieved this goal, and are working towards a more modest target of a terminal installed on each floor of buildings where translators work. Other problems confronting us early in the period after delivery of the software included the need for selectivity in data retrieval. We had massive quantities of old terminology on paper cards – archive material if you like. Each division wanted to transfer its own archives to the computer. This carried with it the risk of nine–times duplication. To mitigate the effects of such duplication, a strategy was devised which would enable any division consulting the computer to see its own material first in answer to an enquiry, and only subsequently see other divisions' material.

THE CONFIDENCE CODE

The confidence code was to be achieved via a confidence code management system. On input, divisions could classify their material with one of three confidence codes. Confidence code 3 indicates that the record is worthy of appearing in a published glossary. When I say the record is worthy, what I am really assessing is the quality of the translation path from the foreign language to the mother tongue. Confidence code 2 indicates that the translation path has been approved by a terminologist and code 1 indicates a suggestion emanating from a translator – this does not imply that terminologists know a lot more than translators, but simply that terminologists are given the time to explore terminological problems, whereas translators are not. Finally there is confidence code Ø (zero) which designates what we call a system-established inversion of terminology. That is to say, the system has located a record containing the search term and a possible translation, but the translation path has not been established by a linguist in the required direction.

Illustration of inversion

For example, the English Division might have come across the Belgian expression '*tapis plain*' in a text describing our new building in Brussels. Every office must have a '*tapis plain*' – and the translator will happily translate this as 'fitted carpet'. In turn, the terminologist can give the translation path from French into English confidence code 3. However, if the French Division had to translate an English document containing the term 'fitted carpet', they could not happily put down in their texts '*tapis plain*' since '*tapis plain*' is a Belgicism, and standard French prefers '*moquette*'.

I hope that this example demonstrates how the confidence code system works in practice. It informs translators working into a particular language that data bearing a high confidence code has been approved by the terminologists of that division, whilst at the same time giving them full access, though lower down the card pile, to data approved in the reverse direction by other divisions. What one might call a multi-bilingual system. Naturally if, having consulted the record, the terminologist is able to add his own missing language, he will do so. In this way, the system should gradually grow into an eleven-language system where the more important records all have the full eleven languages recorded on them.

This brings me to another specific feature of the system. Traditional large computerised databanks had to be – and still probably have to be – loaded by people specialising in data capture. What we wanted for our system was that, ideally, any translator – and certainly any terminologist – could at any time of the day sit down in front of a terminal and type in the data for a new card or add his or her language to an existing record, confident in the knowledge that within a matter of hours that data would form part of the main databank. We did not want to wait for weeks for data to be processed by specialists.

HOW TERMINOLOGY PROBLEMS ARISE

This requirement reflected one crucial aspect of our work. We are usually in our nine language divisions simultaneously translating the same difficult documents and encountering linguistic problems at the same points. Typically, the contact between translator and terminologist is face-to-face. The translator walks into the terminology office, gives you a photocopy of the offending page, and expects a telephone call within the next ten minutes with a translation of the problem term. Now, if one terminologist has solved the problem, it is desirable that the information he or she has unearthed should be made available to other Council translators as soon as possible. This information could be a reference in Community legislation, a previous document dealing with the same subject, or a full definition in the source language of what the technical term means. Even a translation into a third language can be useful if the translator is more familiar with the term in that language than in the one from which he or she is translating. And, as I stated earlier, speed is of the essence.

SIMPLICITY OF CONSULTATION

From the outset, we wanted translators to be able to consult the databank without more than half an hour's prior training being necessary. A large degree of automation was therefore requested. It was part of the system definition that an English translator would be able to stand at a logged-in terminal, type a French word and get answers in English, that a German would be able to type the French word and get answers from the terminal in German, and so on. In other words that the users, once they had declared themselves to the system, would have a number of defaults, i.e. a number of automatic assumptions, associated with their username. This has been achieved. The system does indeed respond according to the identity of the enquirer.

However, it is clear that translators will sometimes want to make enquiries in other languages. Changing source languages – or problem languages, as the system calls them – is also easy. The codes are similar to those in Eurodicautom.

DISPLAY FORMATS

Much discussion went into the design of the display formats, that is the way the system actually looks on the video screens. I personally would have liked to employ the services of a graphic artist, but our budget did not stretch to that! So compromises were hammered out between the users and the programmers. I might add that the user group is mainly to blame for the ensuing result.

The system usually displays what we call the restricted format. This is designed to give the data of a bilingual record as one screenful. Also available from menus – that is, option lists at the end of each display – are the full format and the summary format. The full format is archival and hence designed for the use of full-time terminologists. The summary format gives a minimum of information and is suitable for browsing. It is possible to give a command to the system to impose one of these two formats for a session instead of the usual restricted format. We arrived at three different display formats because the individual requirements of the different language divisions could not be reconciled.

MY OWN ROLE

I should now like to go into somewhat greater detail about my own involvement in the project. About two years ago I was elected by my fellow terminologists to the TIS Liaison Group, given the task of liaising with the ICL staff resident in the building on the development and enhancement of the system. There was and there continues to be a learning process on both sides. The ICL staff and myself share English as a mother tongue. I think it would have been much more difficult to achieve progress with this project if at least one of the Liaison Group had not spoken the same mother tongue as the computing team. When experts from two different areas – computing and languages – come together they have to learn something about each other's subjects in order to communicate effectively and to avoid disastrous misunderstandings. Two years ago I knew nothing at all about computers. Three or four years ago I suspect that at least some of the ICL team knew very little about the problems of sorting words in the Danish alphabet or the manner in which the Irish language inflects. We have both had to learn. Although computing to an outsider seems to be a forbidding fortress, defended by incomprehensible vocabulary, although it seems to be a totally closed world, I can assure you – even if you are only beginning to tackle it at home with a personal computer or word processor – that perseverance pays dividends and that there are little doorways in the curtain wall of the fortress. (Such doorways are the 'Tandy' series of books on data processing, and the better written system manuals [4]). The technical side – the underlying science – is extremely sophisticated and complicated and I would not pretend to have done more than scratch the surface of it in what I have learned. But the concepts which enable you to understand what a computer can and what it cannot do, or what your particular computer can or cannot do, are not so difficult.

PRACTICAL CONCLUSIONS

There are several important practical conclusions I can draw from my experiences. When staff assure you that the computer can do something, it does not mean that it can do it tomorrow. Often what you have said you want the computer to do needs much more careful definition if you are to have the results you hope for. Words as data are much more manageable and can be manipulated in many more ways if from the outset you have defined clearly what you expect to do with that data, and how you wish to extract or reconstitute it. You must specify what you want to be able to search for, what you wish to be linked. A computer cannot jump to conclusions in the way the human mind can. At a very elementary level, it is obvious that the words in the computer are just binary code (i.e. long figures made up of off and on signals) and, to give these figures all the associations you want them to have, they must be put into categories – they have to be tagged, marked, tied down in various ways.

In a terminology database, careful thought needs to be given to questions such as – Do you really want the computer to search on empty words such as '*de*' in French, or 'the' in English?

If you are putting together a database, how do you want it to handle apostrophes? Make sure you understand how it will deal with them – and the effect this will have on searches. And what about plurals? We use a truncation character to help cope with plurals when searching.

SUBJECT CODING

If you decide to categorise your words with a subject code system, make sure you do not invent a system which is so complicated that nobody will ever use it. We decided not to go for any universal theoretical systems, but simply use the subject codes that appear on our documents in any case – abbreviations like AGRI for Agriculture and CONSOM for Consumer Affairs. Yes, we ended up with an English system using French subject codes, but at least the codes have a mnemonic quality. The main thing is that we find them easy to work with, and ease of use in the work situation is of far greater importance to us than any theoretical precision.

MISTAKES

We have of course made mistakes too. Nobody in the early stages of the project gave sufficient attention to the fact that people like to keep monolingual data, records of expressions they have come across in their reading with associated contexts and definitions, which in the immediate future are unlikely to be translated, e.g. someone might wish to enter the expressions 'community charge' or 'poll tax'. We have had to solve this problem in a rather ad hoc manner. Monolingual words are assumed to be translations from Latin with the Latin field left empty. Currently, such cards cause the database to lock up; ICL are attending to the problem as a matter of urgency.

GLOSSARIES

An early requirement of the system was that it should produce glossaries automatically. Not quite at the touch of a button, with a leather-bound volume coming out of the laser printer, but tending that way. The glossary part of the project for some reason always seems to be subject to postponement. Recent budgetary problems have cast their shadow over the glossaries question, but there is some hope that coding will be begun soon.

In the first stage, we hope to produce bilingual glossaries. The material will be selected from the database using the confidence codes and, if required, subject codes. For example, it should be easily possible to produce a listing of terms relating to fisheries: subject code PECHE.

The automatic generation of headwords in the glossary is a major problem. Understandably, it has been the task of the linguists to define what a headword is. I have had some very, very tiring evenings trying to define what a headword is. But if we as language experts cannot define what we mean by headwords we can hardly expect the computer expert to produce software that carefully prints them. So we have to rise to the challenge.

AFTER-SALES SERVICE AND SUPPORT

Is any of this of use to people working at home with their own personal computers? I think the lessons to be learned are that when buying computer equipment you should examine the quality of the manuals as much as − yes, quite as much as − the quality of what the salesman can demonstrate to you. See where your information is going to come from the second you have handed your money over. In this respect we have had excellent support from ICL and from Ace Computer Systems, who produce some of our word processing software. Make sure that you do not take too many things for granted. Linguists assume that everybody understands their special requirements as regards character sets, their need to be able to use a wide variety of symbols, perhaps their requirements for a certain type of keyboard, their assumptions that what they type will be what they see on the screen, will be what they can print. I'm afraid it ain't necessarily so. Be prepared to use the programs supplied to you in an adventurous manner. A lot of the better computer software can be tailored very closely to your own requirements, if you are prepared to put in the time studying the technical manuals. Then, with a helping hand from the supplier, you can adapt the software to your personal needs. But make sure that you are able to define carefully what your requirements are, and that you have bought equipment that is sufficiently adaptable. Manually produced mock-ups of the output you want to obtain from your computer can greatly aid such definition.

TIS AS A PUBLIC DATABASE

Our computer department informs me that it might be possible for the TIS system to be made available to the general public on subscription terms. However, this is not likely to occur in the very near future since bulk loading of data is not yet completed, and we have not seriously tackled the problem of duplicates.

EQUIPMENT AND SOFTWARE AVAILABLE

Much of the equipment and some of the software we are using are available to the general public. For example, I believe that the Olivetti ETS 2010/S word processor which was originally used as a terminal in the system can still be supplied and, although it takes a lot of mastering as a word processor, it nevertheless has some very unusual features which might fit your requirements for a full European character set. The LEX word processing package of Ace Computer Systems Ltd has been adapted for our use and does support different character sets.

ACKNOWLEDGEMENTS

I would not like to leave you with the impression that I, as a system user, have been responsible for much of the system's design and programming. This has been a description of TIS as seen by a user – the programmers would have another tale to tell. Above all, the finished product is the result of successful teamwork, and without such teamwork the project would have foundered many times over.

REFERENCES

[1]   *Glossaire des Communautés Européennes, anglais–français* (3rd ed.) 1982.
      European Communities glossary, French–English (8th ed.). ISBN 92-824-0131-6.
      Luxembourg: 1984.
      EG-Wörterverzeichnis, Französisch–Deutsch (3rd ed.). ISBN 92-824-0123-5. Lux-
      embourg: 1984.
      EG-Wörterverzeichnis, Deutsch–Französisch. ISBN 92-824-0411-0. Luxembourg:
      1987.
[2]   *Glossaire d'abréviations multilingue.* ISBN 92-824-0115-4. Luxembourg: 1983.
      Glossaire entraves techniques, 1. Procédures administratives. ISBN 92-824-0172-3.
      Luxembourg: 1984.
      Glossaire ACP-CEE (+ Liste des etats). ISBN 92-824-0173-1. Luxembourg: 1984.
      NB Not all these glossaries contain the full range of languages. HMSO is the British
      supplier of Community glossaries.
[3]   See also:
      BROOKS, F.P., Jr. *The mythical man-month. Essays on software engineering.* Reading,
      Massachusetts: Addison-Wesley Publishing Co., 1982. ISBN 0-201-00650-2.
[4]   For example:
      ASCHNER, K., *The word processing handbook.* ISBN 0-330-28535-1. London: Pan
      Books Ltd., 1983.

HAMMOND, R. *The writer and the word processor.* ISBN 0-340-36595-1. Sevenoaks: Hodder and Stoughton, 1984.
MORRIS, S. *Using DOS Plus on the Amstrad PC.* ISBN 1-85181-063-3. Barnet: Glentop Publishers Ltd, 1986.
WALKER, R.S. *Understanding computer science,* Vol. I. Fort Worth: Radio Shack (Tandy Corporation), 1981.

Evaluation of software and hardware for multilingual text production

Keith Adkins

The College of Ripon and York St John, York, UK

The paper first considers the basic differences which exist between available computers, word processing programs and printers, in order to arrive at criteria which might be used in selecting a system which provides those facilities which would be of importance to the translator, and includes a discussion of how a system can most effectively be adapted to particular needs and preferences. An example is described in which the author adapted a package for use by trainee translators in the Department of Modern Languages at Salford University. More recent software and hardware developments are also discussed, particularly desktop publishing and the laser printer, where falling prices make it likely that their use by translators will become more widespread in the near future.

It seems that an ever-increasing number of translators are giving up the typewriter for the word processor and are realising that this leads to economies of time in text production and revision, as well as to a better presented end product. Generally popular among freelance translators in Great Britain is the Amstrad PCW256 computer, running Locoscript software. Since the PCW256 and its associated software came on to the market there have been various developments in text production hardware and software on small computers, including the entirely new addition of desktop publishing packages, which permit an even higher standard of text production.

Text production packages available today differ greatly in the range of facilities offered, but the basic requirement of the user is clearly that they should allow him or her to produce exactly what is wanted, and to produce it as easily and as quickly as possible. The translator may be content with the system he or she is using at present but would be well advised to be aware of the alternatives which are constantly becoming available. There is clearly no need to update one's system for the sake of doing so but, on the other hand, the fact that a certain system best suited one's requirements five years ago does not mean that the same is necessarily true now.

The disincentives to change – cost, time to learn a new system, and possible problems of not being able to reuse old files – may be outweighed by the advantages. There is a need to stand back and ask if one is using the right equipment for what one is doing. For example, if the type of translation work one does frequently requires the drawing of boxes around tables, or the compilation of indexes for books, a simple word processor may no longer be the right tool to use. Recent improvements in hardware and software mean one can do more, and that one can do things more quickly and easily. Moreover, a more powerful system is not necessarily more difficult to learn or to use. A system offering many of the features discussed in this paper can cost around £1,500 (plus printer) which may be considered to be within the price range of the small business user.

This paper seeks to survey the main features of hardware and software currently available for text production using computers, focusing on both word processing (WP) and desktop publishing (DTP) packages. The discussion will be aimed at the freelance translator, with a limited budget, who will be working on a small computer system.

RECENT DEVELOPMENTS

In order to set in context the range of possibilities offered by currently available text production software I shall briefly describe a number of developments, mainly in hardware, which have taken place over the last few years and are still continuing apace today. These developments have a direct impact upon the kinds and quality of software which can be used.

More powerful microprocessors

The last few years have seen a development away from the early microprocessors used in home computers, such as the Z80, found in the Amstrad CPC6128 and PCW256, and the 6502, found in the Apple and BBC computers. From about 1982 onwards these were being superseded by machines based on the 8088 processor, principally the IBM PC-compatibles. From about 1984/5 we have seen the arrival of computers based on the 80286 and 68000 processors such as the Apple Macintosh, Atari ST and PC-AT generation of machines.

Computers based on the earlier microprocessors were limited in the amount of memory (64 kilobytes) which could be used easily and effectively by programs, compared to those based on more recent processors, where 512 kilobytes is now considered the basic minimum requirement. In addition, the speed of the processors has increased, so that more sophisticated programs can be used, without the user having to wait an unacceptably long time for them to carry out complex operations such as changing page layouts or reformatting long documents. It is even possible to run several programs at once, to allow, for example, immediate access to a database while word processing.

Decrease in the price of laser printers

Laser printers are gaining wide recognition as combining the advantages of the daisywheel and the dot matrix printers, while avoiding the disadvantages of both. Their price has been steadily falling so that the cost of some of those currently available is down to below £1,500. The laser printer produces excellent quality print – no longer does a text have to look as though it was produced on a word processor – and permits the use of many different fonts (i.e. character sizes, character faces, and types of emphasis), as well as graphics for the production of diagrams and pictures. It also has the advantage of being quiet in operation. Printing speed depends on the complexity of the page, for example on the number of changes of font on the page and on whether graphics are present, but for normal text it is several pages per minute.

The flexibility of the laser printer, and its wider availability following the decrease in its price, has led to the proliferation of desktop publishing software (to be described later) and to the addition of extra features to the more powerful word processing packages, in order to better exploit its power. Thus, even those who cannot yet afford a laser printer can make use of the software and have the text printed or typeset from their discs by one of the many firms now offering such a service.

Decrease in the price of hard disc drives

Hard discs, unlike floppy discs, are permanently fixed into the machine and give a storage capacity of at least twenty times that of floppy discs, as well as much faster access to the disc contents. This means that much larger programs can be used, such as those for desktop publishing. The memory of the computer cannot contain the whole of such a program, but instead reads in parts of the program from the hard disc as required. In addition, desktop publishing programs need a large quantity of storage space for files and for fonts, and for this the smaller capacity of floppy discs is much less convenient. The smallest hard disc drives currently cost about £200.

Improved quality of screen display

The improvements in the resolution of screens have led to a more acceptable representation on the screen of text and graphics, while improved software techniques have allowed the development of programs which are easier to operate and which extend the possibilities available. For example, in many packages the screen can now be divided into windows through which different documents, or different parts of the same document, or even screens from different programs (for example a word processor and a database), can be viewed at the same time, and menus can be made to pop up instantly where and when required. Options in the program no longer have to be selected by typing in on the keyboard: instead a mouse (a hand-held device which is moved about on a flat surface in order to move a pointer around the screen) makes working much easier and faster, by allowing, for example, very fast editing and selection from menus.

DOCUMENT PRODUCTION SOFTWARE

Having briefly reviewed the trends of the last few years we shall now look at the different types of document production software currently available.

There are two types of software available for producing documents: word processing (WP) packages and desktop publishing (DTP) packages, about ten and two years old respectively. The distinction between the two is becoming increasingly blurred, as many of the facilities provided by DTP packages are also available on the more powerful WP packages; DTP packages thus really, to some extent, provide an extension of the facilities offered by WP packages.

For those who may be unfamiliar with such packages we can first give a summary of what each of them allows one to do, followed by discussion of points to be borne in mind when evaluating both the hardware and software, and a table of the main features that text-production packages are able to provide and which should be considered by the prospective user.

WP packages basically allow the user to enter and edit text; to set character formats (fonts), paragraph formats (e.g. indentation, justification, line spacing) and page layout (e.g. margins, running heads, page numbering); to print text; and to store text on a disc for future use.

It is usually considered that DTP packages allow for the final preparation of documents to a standard appropriate for publication, by reading in text produced by a word processor, and graphics produced by a drawing program or from a scanner, and by enabling final editing of the text and graphics and allowing the document to be manipulated and the page layout arranged as required.

The translator may be particularly interested in certain features of DTP packages which are not available in WP packages: a wider choice of fonts, and more powerful facilities for page layout (e.g. more than one column) and paragraph format (e.g. highlighting and variable line spacing); proportional spacing of characters; editing on the screen of the exact form the document will have when printed out; the incorporation of drawings and pictures into the document; and the production of tables of contents and indexes.

DTP packages currently available tend to fall into two groups: some are better for producing short documents such as newsletters, sales brochures and magazines requiring complicated page layouts. Examples are XPress, Pagemaker, and Ready Set Go 3. Others are better for producing books, where standard page layouts, headings and subheadings are required, together with the generation of tables of contents and indexes. Ventura is a DTP package of this type.

WHAT TO LOOK FOR

There are now many packages of both types on the market and when assessing which might be of particular use to one's own working needs the following are points to be borne in mind.

The facility of a mouse is in many ways preferable to using the keyboard. Editing with a mouse is faster than with the keyboard and other facilities are easier to use if accessed from menus using a mouse, rather than by typing in commands. This also means that one does not have to remember the commands, which can be a problem if you use the package infrequently or if you use a powerful package with many facilities.

The system must clearly be able to produce on the screen and on the printer all the characters and print features needed. Systems vary in what characters can be produced and in how easy it is to produce them. For example, the IBM PC and compatibles are supplied with software for changing the keyboard into any one of a number of different European keyboards. However, some of the accented characters may still not be accessible using a single keystroke and have to be entered by typing in the appropriate numeric code (a two- or three-digit number). Although DTP packages and laser printers are both capable in principle of working with any required character set, the software to allow, for example, Cyrillic or Greek script to be used is not yet generally available.

Editing a document into precisely the form wanted is clearly much easier if its appearance, as it is edited on the screen, matches as closely as possible the appearance of the printed product. Character fonts, emphasis, page breaks, right-justification, page numbers, running heads, and true line spacing, for example, are not shown correctly on the screen on many WP packages, whereas they tend to be shown by DTP packages.

There should obviously be a clear manual, and a tutorial on disc or on paper can be very useful in getting to know a package. A quick-reference guide on paper, or on the screen, to the keys needed for each function is useful, but most important is the ability to call up help on the screen at any time on any intended task or on the task you are in the middle of.

The quality of the file saving or loading facilities varies greatly. It should obviously not be possible to lose text, for example by quitting without saving or by not noticing that a 'disc full' message appeared when you tried to save text. A catalogue of files on disc, to be selected from, should be given when loading and saving.

Turning to more specific features, Table 1 lists the main features that many text production packages currently provide and which should be considered by the prospective user. The table begins with some basic features that, surprisingly, are often missing from some of the less sophisticated packages and moves towards more advanced features that are only available in the more powerful DTP packages.

IS THERE ANYTHING THAT WP AND DTP PACKAGES CANNOT DO?

Perhaps the one disadvantage, from the user's point of view, of the most recently developed WP and DTP packages, is that their programs cannot be entered in order to tune them more closely to individual needs. The Tasword WP package on the Amstrad CPC6128 computer is a single program which nevertheless allows

Table 1. Main features of a text production package

Undoing last operation	This refers to the ability to reverse the last operation carried out, most importantly the accidental deletion of text.
Showing current position in text	An indication of the position of page breaks allows checking that breaks do not occur in unwanted places (e.g. in the middle of a table), while a display of current page and line numbers permits cross-referencing, for example.
Storing rulers	If the positions of margins, indents and tab stops for each paragraph are remembered they do not need to be set up again when editing.
Proper tabs	Text aligned on tab stops should move when the tap stops are moved, to allow, for example, the widths of columns in a table to be changed.
Word count	Keeps a running count of the number of words in a document.
Hard carriage return	Paragraphs not separated by a blank line (e.g. lines of an address or a table) should not be combined into one paragraph on reformatting.
Hard space	Spaces typed in should be left in, and not lost, on reformatting (e.g. double spaces between sentences).
Non-break character	This refers to a character which can be placed between two words and which will print as a space, but which will prevent the words being split between two lines (e.g. for names).
Split-screen editing	This allows the screen to be divided into separate areas to allow more than one document to be seen simultaneously.
Repeated text facilities	This refers to short-cut methods available for entering words, phrases, or sentences which occur frequently, using only one or two key presses.
Notepad	This is an area where reminders of things to be looked up, or things to be inserted later in a document, can be temporarily stored.
Hyphenation	Words can be automatically hyphenated if they occur near the end of a line, with the ability to specify words (e.g. names) which are not to be hyphenated.
Intelligent placing of page breaks	This usually refers to the automatic avoidance of single lines of paragraphs at the tops and bottoms of pages.
Spelling check	This may be done as you type or after typing. Words can be added to the dictionary used.
Thesaurus	Gives synonyms and antonyms of any word.
Linking with other packages	For example, with a database for terminology or for names and addresses for a circular letter.
Standard document templates	Templates giving page and paragraph layouts, and character fonts for headings and subheadings, can be set up for different kinds of documents and saved, to avoid repeating the setting-up process.

Text in multiple columns	This allows text in any number of columns, with any spacing between columns.
Automatic paragraph numbering and emphasis	For example, highlighting may be by a large dot or other character at the left, or by adding boxes around areas of text, or by using horizontal or vertical lines.
Incorporation of graphics	Pictures and diagrams can be produced using a drawing package or by a scanner, with the size and position changed, and text run around them.
Reduced view	This allows a whole page, or two facing pages, to be viewed at once to judge the appearance of the page layout.
Left and right page features	These allow different margins for binding, different positions of page numbers or different running heads on left- and right-hand pages.
Proportional spacing	For high quality work each character is allocated an appropriate width and the blank space on each line carefully divided up.
Linking documents	The chapters of a book, for example, are usually printed from separate files, but with a consistent layout, consecutive page numbering, and a table of contents and index produced.
Table of contents	Headings and subheadings can be taken automatically from the chapter files, the correct page numbers added, and the table set out in a specified way.
Index	Items for inclusion can be marked and the index is automatically created with correct page numbering.
Footnotes	Markers can be inserted in the text and the corresponding footnotes typed in. On printing each footnote will be fitted on the same page as the reference to it.

extensive customisation to be carried out. An example of what is possible is the customisation carried out by the author for use by trainee translators at the University of Salford to permit them to work in French, Spanish, Portuguese, Italian, German, Danish and Swedish. The resulting adaptation provided the facility to type in, see displayed on the screen and subsequently print all the characters needed, both lower and upper case. In addition, the commonly used accented characters for each language were assigned to the keys of the numeric pad, for ease of use. Such a customisation allows for the creation of characters not included in the original WP package; hence Cyrillic or Greek script, for example, could also have been added if it had been required.

Having said that, it has to be borne in mind that many of the packages now available will do much that such a simple system as the Amstrad CPC6128 plus Tasword cannot do.

A CHANGING ATTITUDE OF MIND?

Translators over the present decade have for the most part shown great adaptability in going over in such large numbers, and generally with some enthusiasm, to using a word processor. Initially this has demanded a large input of time in learning the chosen system, and perhaps in customising it to the individual translator's requirements. Naturally enough this has resulted in a fierce devotion to the system one has become familiar with through so much burning of the midnight oil.

As the decade draws to a close it is perhaps time to take stock of the demands of one's current translation work in terms of the type, range and quality of presentation required by the customer, or soon to be required as more advanced technology becomes cheaper and more widely used. For example, the users of translations will increasingly demand camera-ready copy, or material on disc for a typesetting machine, and for the competitive translator, quality of presentation will become an increasing priority. A dispassionate appraisal may lead to a realisation of the shortcomings of the systems devised in the early 1980s for the beginnings of the home computer revolution.

Translators–and indeed all professional producers of text–may need to adopt a more throw-away attitude, indeed the attitude already adopted with regard to television sets, radios and cars. Regular capital investment in re-equipping, a recognised necessity of most business ventures, should perhaps be built into the translator's costings. Aspects of the translation and text-production task should thus become simpler and quicker, while camera-ready text produced as standard should command higher rates from many users, or cut out the translator's need to resort to secretarial services. If we couple this with the fact that learning to use a new program becomes easier with each one learned, we can perhaps begin to be less daunted by the prospect.

Session 2: Report of discussion

Rapporteur: Guyonne Proudlock, freelance translator

Regarding the back-up service given by suppliers of software and hardware, Robert Dewsnap asked Dr Adkins if it was fair to say that the quality of back-up service was proportional to the amount of money which had been spent on it and that if one bought a cheap package one got less help after purchase. Dr Adkins thought this was not necessarily the case; however, in Chris Burdon's opinion one should not expect the same service from cut-price high street shops. Mrs Myriam Paish (Wimborne) supported that opinion in the light of her own experience and stressed the importance of choosing suppliers who would provide a good back-up service.

Mr Navid Babar (Sheffield City Council) asked Dr Adkins if he had looked into the adaptation of word processors to oriental languages, to which he replied that although he had not, he could see no reason why it should not be possible to produce any character. Chris Burdon remarked that at the Council of Ministers characters could be created or modified on screen by the users but that laser printers were needed to print them. This of course was very costly. Mr Babar asked Mr Forrest of ICL if ICL were considering the question of oriental languages. Mr Forrest replied that although ICL products were very much geared to Europe, Arabic was completely covered but not yet Chinese. He added that the incorporation of total character sets ran the supplier into millions of pounds. Douglas Clarke of the Cranfield Institute of Technology mentioned that a system had been developed at Cranfield for the input of Chinese characters into a terminal with a QWERTY keyboard. Addressing Dr Adkins, he commented on future trends for WPs. In his opinion, they would eventually incorporate far more linguistic analysis, such as a syntactic analyser which would point out to the user any existing syntactic ambiguities in the source document, thus reducing the number of potential errors before the document even reached the translator's desk.

Mrs Lisa Suscenko (London), who translates into and out of Russian, enquired whether Locoscript 2 could be used on Telecom Gold while retaining the full character set. Chris Burdon felt that this did not represent a problem as the ASCII set was extendable. At the Council of Ministers, GPO lines were used to run their system which was converted into the ASCII set for transmission.

In answer to a question from Angelika Jaeger (Frankfurt), Chris Burdon mentioned that the Council of Ministers' termbank TIS was not yet available online but he hoped that it would be in the near future.

Remarking that word processing hardware and software was in his opinion very costly, Gordon Stuart (Scotland) asked whether these aids for multi-lingual character sets could be made available for the electronic typewriter and whether Eurodicautom and other termbanks could be made available on facsimile. Chris Burdon felt that Fax would be inappropriate but that they were likely to become available on CD-ROM.

Claude Fleurent then called for translators to use equipment which was IBM compatible. This was extremely important from the client's point of view. He added that industry as a client was prepared to pay a realistic fee for such a service, including a percentage towards the cost and depreciation of suitable hardware and software. Florence Herbulot (Paris) remarked that there was a danger that translators might be judged on the compatibility of their equipment and the quality of presentation and that the client might not pay sufficient attention to the essential criterion: the quality of the translation itself.

Finally, in response to Pamela Mayorcas' comment that the Amstrad PCW did seem to provide inexpensively a great number of useful features, Francine Cronin (London) asked what efforts had been made by the profession, through ITI, to bring about the last few necessary improvements to the Amstrad PCW. Pamela replied that Roger L'Estrange had tried to make some contact with Amstrad in the early days of ITI, without success however. She suggested that the attempt be renewed, particularly now that ITI was gaining influence in the translation world. This could possibly take the form of a jointly drafted set of comments.

Session 3: Training

Chaired by Hugh Keith

Twenty-one years of the postgraduate course at Bath. General considerations on the training of linguists for the 1990s

Michael Croft

University of Bath, UK

The paper attempts to review some of the central problems involved in training linguists in the United Kingdom. A number of these problems have received individual attention in recent conferences, but this author feels that it would be helpful to take a broad overview, in order both to perceive the range and diversity of these issues and to assess the impact of the multiplicity of choices which face those trying to run courses in the present climate of uncertainty and cutbacks.

When I was asked to contribute a paper to this session of the ITI Conference the new academic year had only just begun with its flurry of meetings to discuss future plans and current threats to this or that activity. It was an appropriate time to take stock of the postgraduate course at Bath, if only because nothing we do can be taken for granted, however worthwhile it may seem, or however relevant to the presumed needs of a modern civilised society. The following considerations should be seen, therefore, in that context of continuing debate and evaluation, but they should also, I hope, have a wider relevance than just to the Bath course. I should stress here at the outset that my approach is more strategic than methodological. The background of twenty-one years of experience in running a postgraduate course for intending professional linguists may have provided a clearer view of some of the problems, issues and objectives but it has not given an insight into all the answers.

BASIC PARAMETERS

Some of the most interesting questions one can ask when embarking on a review of this kind are the really basic ones. In considering possible models for training linguists, should we, for instance, aim for an undergraduate or postgraduate course? The pioneers in the field initiated undergraduate studies at the end of the Second World War. Their aims were to identify the skills and abilities as well as the general cultural baggage necessary for such employment, and then to teach and train systematically in those elements. This model for training has dominated the field throughout Continental Europe as well as in Scotland, which in so many educational matters prefers to look across the Channel for inspiration rather than to England.

The advantages of this approach are easily apparent: it is far less haphazard to train peopole for general or specific competences right from school; difficult skills like interpreting can be prepared and taught over a long period and in a carefully graduated manner. But the Continental schools of interpreting and translating do have their critics and there are some drawbacks to their system. Can we be sure that we can identify the most important desiderata? Do we have a clear idea of the sort of general culture we expect in such graduates? How quickly can we react to changing demands or circumstances in a three, four or five year course? How do we estimate intake targets for such degrees or diplomas? Do we plan on the basis of perceived need for graduates or on our capacity to recruit or to teach? It is an all too common occurrence in education for the student numbers to be set as a function of overall intake targets for an institution based on that institution's staffing levels rather than on a clear and informed analysis of the employment market. Where external factors are taken into account they are usually those of student applications and the quality of those applicants. To underestimate the potential market for graduate linguists is not a serious mistake, except for the health of the economy of the country and the quality of the work produced by underqualified translators. If we overestimate, however, we find that we have expensively trained linguists with no vocation to go to.

STANDARDS

The question of standards is also problematical. How can we be sure that all our graduates are sufficiently competent to work professionally? One solution is to follow the path of other professions such as engineering and develop a system of accreditation by the professional bodies. This may well be the path down which we in the United Kingdom should be going. The inevitable consequence, however, of the active participation of such bodies or of the main employers of linguists is a significant failure rate. The number of failures may often be a function of the state of the employment market rather than of absolute standards. Indeed, in some Continental schools the pass rate is lower than the failure rate at certain stages.

If the first degree is not the ideal solution neither is the postgraduate course. The most obvious shortcoming is the limited time at one's disposal to convert graduates with very diverse backgrounds into skilled practitioners. In most cases these graduates will have studied languages up to degree level, although the possession of a modern languages degree is not the only possible requirement.

One thing is certain, the British education system rarely produces technical or scientific graduates with adequate foreign language skills. If one is to consider training linguists and other specialists together on the same course, then only by chance or accident of birth will the non-linguist reach the necessary level of language competence for entry.

I am in danger of getting ahead of myself here, because there already appears to be some kind of implicit assumption creeping in about the skills and level of language competence required. Such assumptions should only be made, however, when we know precisely what our objectives are. Obviously, maximum possible language competence is desirable but there are many additional factors to be considered. Is the course to be for translators or interpreters? What kinds of translating or interpreting might be offered? Translating is a broad enough field, but just think how many different kinds of interpreters there are! The basic requirements of their individual professions, whether it be as community interpreters, court interpreters or those working in conferences, surely demand specialised training programmes. There are crucially different demands to be met, not least in the choice of languages offered and the fields of knowledge explored. I very much doubt whether it makes sense to try to combine such activities under one umbrella despite the economic attractions of large-scale courses.

MARKET NEEDS

The essential point that I am making is that we need to define our objectives very clearly in terms of the market, the types of work our students are going to find. That presupposes a knowledge of that market and of its needs both now and in the future. Such knowledge is easier to come by in some areas than in others, although even in the case of sectors as apparently transparent as the international organisations the messages received are sometimes ambiguous. I have been listening to people from the Language Services of the European Communities for most of the twenty-one years referred to in my title. The only clear message I have been able to discern is that they are usually on the brink of chaos and the flavour of the month is the latest language to join! Planning ahead is not possible because they cannot employ linguists for a new language until that language becomes an official working one. At which moment the floodgates open because the new Member State has a vast backlog of information and legislation to translate as well as new officials and MEP's eager to air their views in an exciting new forum.

Even within the EC, different institutions have quite different language needs. In the Parliament all working languages are regularly in demand and therefore for its Interpretation Service it sometimes seems to be a question of 'never mind the quality, feel the width'. If an aspiring interpreter can offer four languages one sometimes gets the impression that standards are allowed to drop, particularly if one of those languages is, say, Greek or Portuguese. Translators in the English Division of the Commission, by contrast, have occasionally been heard to complain that they rarely get an opportunity to practise any language other than French. Perhaps I am exaggerating slightly, but the essence of my argument is that needs analysis is not quite as simple a process as one might think. As Professor Nigel Reeves of Surrey University has demonstrated on many occasions over the last decade or so, it is no easy matter to get a sensible answer from British industry on this question either. In many cases no thought has been given to likely needs for linguists nor has there been any consideration of how the European Single Market will affect the amount of translation work or the demand for interpreting services. It is a sad but unsurprising comment on our political leaders' awareness that the glossy brochure produced by the DTI to accompany their briefing breakfasts for dynamic British business people explaining how 1992 will affect their lives contains not one mention of the need for foreign languages!

The kind of evidence we have is largely drawn from surveys conducted by the bodies representing linguists. This work is very valuable, particularly since it is frequently concerned with eliciting information about remuneration and working conditions as part of their campaign to improve the status of their professions. By its very nature though, it does not provide course designers with enough data about future needs.

The choice of market is therefore dictated by informed guesswork supported by direct access through one or more individuals to a particular sector or sectors. At Bath the initial impetus came from Professor Coveney's experience of the international organisations. Similar kinds of personal contact have, I believe, underpinned other successful enterprises. For, however confident one may be in the excellence of a course, there can be no progress without regular feedback and, I would argue, constant involvement of professionals in the teaching and programme design. This may sound rather pragmatic, and certain academics will deplore the lack of a firm foundation in theory, particularly translation theory and contrastive linguistics. In an undergraduate course such elements are essential, but at postgraduate level time is short and pressures of all kinds force us to take a less expansive view. One might also argue that graduates should already have a fair grounding in linguistics, although I admit that this is not an entirely satisfactory response.

SELECTION

There is no doubt that selection policy has an impact on course content. The greatest advantage of the postgraduate course is that time and four years of study and experience have combined to narrow the field of applicants to those who are, or should be, both competent linguists and well motivated to become professionals. The question of high linguistic competence is vital. It is not reasonable to expect translating skills to develop or interpreting even to be possible with incomplete knowledge of the languages involved. The most neglected aspect and yet the *sine qua non* for both activities is the perfect command of the target language. Any process of selection must try to identify people who can use English fluently and elegantly under pressure, if English is to be the predominant target language for the course.

WHICH LANGUAGES?

In a sense the question of which foreign languages to offer has already been partly answered earlier in my discussion. The choice of a particular market is one factor, the availability of teaching staff, and the quality of prospective students are also determining elements. There is little point in trying to train translators in languages which have been inadequately learned as I said a moment ago. There may be a place for some training in the more exotic languages, if time and resources permit, but this should only be attempted with linguists who already have proven translating or interpreting skills in other languages.

Our experience together with Professor Reeves' research suggests that the most important languages for commercial, industrial and international organisation requirements will remain as follows: French, German, Spanish, Italian, Arabic and Japanese. There will also be sporadic demand for all the other EC languages and a small but consistent market for high quality Russian. I should stress that my frame of reference is the commercial and conference circuit and not court or Community interpreting.

WHAT SKILLS?

Identifying the skills demanded by the different activities of translating and interpreting prompts the obvious initial question, should we try to cover both together? There are good reasons why they should be separated, not the least being the fact that many students have made up their minds which they wish to pursue. Greater emphasis can be placed on the selection of appropriate candidates if one can identify certain benchmarks for interpreters, for example. Interesting research has been conducted along these lines, but I am not sure that the results have been conclusive. Yet time, as I keep repeating, is of the essence, so narrowing one's objectives must be a sensible option.

On the other side the arguments are not without some force. If the recruitment net can be cast a little wider to encompass people who have not made up their minds or who would like to try interpreting even if they suspect translating is more likely to be their forte, then one can demand higher standards. In addition some authorities believe that translating can be a valuable discipline and preparation for interpreters. This is particularly the case if working within the same organisation, when the thorough familiarity with terminology gained in a translation unit can usefully be transferred to other purposes. One might also add, perhaps a little mischievously, that it would do no harm to some interpreters to have to submit to the greater discipline of written work. Conversely, experience of the intellectual demands of high level interpreting can be a stimulating change from the routine grind of much translation work. Nor it is unknown for translators to be called upon to act as interpreters even in international organisations. As long as people are not unduly penalised on a course for not having skills that they did not really expect were within their grasp, I feel that combining the two can be worthwhile. The main purpose, after all, is to encourage potential and not to punish shortcomings.

Such a choice does, however, have implications for the selection process. The qualities required of an interpreter are not that simple to isolate or devise tests for. Various attempts have been made to establish a profile of the interpreter-type, as I mentioned a little while ago, and august bodies such as AIIC have listed the attributes required of the interpreter. The list is not particularly helpful in the event, since it reads rather like a description of the perfect human being. Maybe AIIC are trying to be constructive, but a sceptical person might get the impression that what they are saying between the lines is 'look how brilliant you have to be to be like us!' So testing for potential without actually getting the candidates to do some interpreting, which is hardly fair since most people have never had the chance to try, is not a very scientific process. I make no claim of infallibility for our tests which are as likely to be flawed as anybody else's, but in them we try to aim for comprehension under pressure, ability to synthesise a complex argument quickly, and good, clear English expression. The exercises are a mixture of written to oral, or written to written, and oral to written tests. In this way we hope to find good all-round linguists with possible interpreter potential.

COURSE CONTENT

Once we have selected the students, and I am deliberately leaving an important stage in the process until later, that is the decision on numbers, then the vast range of possibilities for the curriculum must be faced. Other speakers will be addressing some of these issues in far greater detail and my purpose here is to concentrate more on strategic questions so I shall not dwell on specifics, except to remark on the difficulty of getting agreement from many of the employers on precisely what basic practical skills they expect from trainee translators. For example, some are quite categorical that keyboard skills are essential. All translators, they say, type their own work either on a standard electric typewriter, or a word processor. So, we buy expensive word processors and encourage the students to do all their written work on them. But then another employer says equally adamantly, that they have a large typing pool employed to do that. Their translators are expected to dictate all their work and don't we teach students how to use a dictating machine? Yet another will admit that they do actually have one word processor but it is the sole prerogative of their tame computer freak who would not take kindly to a junior trying to 'borrow' it. Indeed, in one international organisation which will remain anonymous longhand is still the standard medium.

After a while you get the impression that this most basic of areas is a bit of a minefield. The fact is, of course, that we have entered the field of internal office politics. The only safe strategy is to warn the students to tread very warily and introduce them to all the possibilities with a particular emphasis on likely future developments, including post-editing and some reassuring words on machine translation. The one general rule that seems to apply is that industrial and commercial enterprises tend to be more technology-minded than the international organisations.

CONSTRAINTS

Regardless of what we may feel is desirable or necessary in the training of future linguists, whether as translators or interpreters, and for reasons of time I have had to leave out most of the interesting methodological considerations, there is a whole area of constraints about which I have remained silent hitherto. These contraints may well render our general thoughts on what is desirable or necessary totally superfluous. The present environment in higher education is now more than ever a determining and restricting factor in the equation. What I say will be all too familiar to the academics here, but is worth rehearsing for the benefit of those who are not trying to work in universities and polytechnics today.

University departments are now to be funded directly and will be run financially as 'cost centres', responsible for their own ever slimmer budgets. These budgets will be allocated on the basis of crude capitation plus some rather more sophisticated factors which decide the level of equipment and consumables largely on the principle of if it is scientific or technological it should have more and if not, bad luck! The obvious and inevitable result of this is that all activities must be seen to be economically viable only in the narrowest sense. That it can be run on a favourable staff/student ratio of at least 1:10 is a basic prerequisite of any course, be it undergraduate or postgraduate. The only exceptions involve overseas students who pay far higher fees and can therefore be accommodated on much more favourable staff/student ratios, perhaps as low as 1:6.

I am not sure what the average number of hours are taught by average lecturers up and down the United Kingdom, nor am I acquainted with the total number of hours taught on the 'average' vocational course. As a very crude guess I should put the range for university lecturers at between 150 and 300 hours and the total input to a one-year course as about twice that. The crude implications of those figures, if they are roughly correct, is that there must be a minimum of twenty students per year on any such course for it to be economically viable. This is not a crippling problem for undergraduate courses where the grant funding is automatic. The situation for postgraduates is quite different. The present system of Department of Education and Science (DES) bursaries, allocated by quota to certain vocational courses, is totally inadequate and the figure of twenty can only be reached at present with a high proportion of self-financing or overseas students. There are implications, however, for both undergraduate and postgraduate courses. The recent University Grants Committee attack on what it calls small departments means that there must be at least four full-time staff members for each language taught, otherwise a department is likely to be closed down as unviable. If, therefore, we wish to cover three or four languages on a course the target number of students in the department in any one year must be at least 120 or 160.

STAFF MOTIVATION

Another interesting factor in the equation is the new system of staff appraisal. Although in the past all staff were expected to contribute according to their talents to the three activities of teaching, administration and research, increasingly in my experience only research is being taken into account. The argument runs roughly like this: all staff teach and we cannot assess that activity without asking the students, which many senior academics seem to be unhappy about, so all we can do is count hours. All staff beyond their probationary period ought to be doing some administration, and anyway all the important administration is done by the central administration, so we cannot take that into account. That leaves research. We cannot measure quality, but we can count money and we can count pages, so at last we have something quantifiable, that will be the criterion. To the casual observer this may seem inoffensive and even mildly diverting, but to the intelligent young lecturer and even to some of the older ones the message is clear. Forget about teaching and particularly forget about teaching anything which is not directly relevant to your own specialist research field.

In a broadly humanistic Arts department the effect of this kind of pressure is very interesting. It means that the traditional type of Arts or Social Science Faculty is encouraged in two directions. First into areas where research funds might be available, and secondly into what one might call pure scholarship. These are excellent in themselves, and I for one am delighted that the prolific researcher into mediaeval literature will be justly rewarded. The other side of the coin, however, is that practical and vocational language teaching with direct relevance for the economic future of the country will be very low in the pecking order.

LACK OF POLICY

I believe that the present environment in higher education will lead to the watering down and possibly the closure of *all* postgraduate courses for professional linguists aimed at UK students within the next five years unless there emerges from somewhere, and preferably from within the DES, a policy on the training of such linguists, which takes account of the needs of the market and of the education system's ability to respond to those needs. The alternative will be an inevitable drift towards the worst aspects of the Continental system with high intakes and correspondingly high failure rates. This may be what we want, but I believe we should think carefully about the consequences. In future most of the choices I have described earlier will be determined by the availability of sufficient numbers of student applicants on the one hand, while the choice of languages taught will be decided on the basis of the availability of locally recruited poorly paid part-time external lecturers. In being responsive to the market we will be responding to pressures within the wrong markets. The bizarre consequence of the DES's attempts to make the education system more effective and more responsive to the needs of society will be to downgrade specialist linguist training in favour of ever more esoteric research in the Arts.

The training of community interpreters

Alastair M. Scouller

Polytechnic of Central London, UK

I should make it clear at the outset that the PCL is not directly concerned with the training of community interpreters at present. I have been involved in a personal capacity in the Community Interpreting Project, run by the Institute of Linguists with the financial support of the Nuffield Foundation. My role in the project has been that of an adviser on interpreting skills, a visiting tutor and an examiner.

THE NEED

The need for community interpreting services is illustrated by the experience of numerous members of ethnic communities within British society, who in their contacts with officialdom at various levels have come up against a blank wall of incomprehension because they are unable to express themselves adequately in English. These people may be members of well-established communities, such as the Italian population in Peterborough, or the Chinese community in the West End of London. In spite of having lived in the United Kingdom for a number of years, many of them, especially in the older generation, have found it difficult or even impossible to learn English. Others may be recent arrivals, from Bangladesh for example, or Vietnam, who have not yet had an opportunity to acquire a sufficient mastery of the host language.

While the need to provide interpreting services may be relatively easy to establish, the need for training may be less obvious. After all, there have always been people within the community who have been prepared to act as intermediaries whenever linguistic problems have arisen. The courts, the police and other agencies have long had lists of persons to call upon in times of need, and many of these people have provided, and still do provide, an excellent and highly professional service. But the system, if indeed it is correct to call it a system at all, has been unreliable. As well as the well qualified and experienced interpreters, use has often been made of waiters, hospital cleaners, or relatives, on the premise that 'anything is better than nothing'.

THE COMMUNITY INTERPRETING PROJECT

It was largely in order to counter this hit-and-miss approach to community interpreting that the Institute of Linguists, with the assistance of my predecessor at the PCL, Professor Pat Longley, set up the Community Interpreting Project (CIP). The idea of this pilot project, which was based in Peterborough and Cambridge, was to demonstrate the advantage of systematic training for community interpreters, drawing on the experience gained, and utilising some of the techniques developed, in the training of conference interpreters at the PCL and elsewhere. My own involvement with the CIP arose more or less by accident in July 1986, when Professor Longley was prevented by illness from attending the course then running in Cambridge, and a number of AIIC colleagues, including myself, stepped in to take her place.

The project was designed to lead to the award of the Certificate in Community Interpreting by the Institute of Linguists. Students were trained and examined in one of three 'bands', or areas of specialisation, as follows:

Band 1 – the legal system
        (lower courts, police, probation service)
Band 2 – social services
        (including local government services, education, welfare, etc.)
Band 3 – the Health Service

The first two courses to be run, in Peterborough and Cambridge, offered training in Band 1. A further course held in Peterborough covered Band 2, and a course currently running at Addenbrooke's Hospital in Cambridge covers Band 3. A course organised in Bedford by the Bedfordshire Industrial Language Training Unit, was not formally part of the project but became closely associated with it, and prepared students to sit the Institute's Certificate examination in Band 2.

SELECTION

The selection of suitable candidates for training as community interpreters is of fundamental importance. Linguistic competence, meaning a high level of proficiency in *both* languages, is clearly essential, but candidates must also show a thorough understanding of the cultural background, some knowledge of the institutional framework within which they will be expected to work, and an ability to learn, as well as possessing the appropriate inter-personal skills and a capacity to deal objectively with highly sensitive issues.

Selection is done by means of a written translation test in both languages and an interview which is also conducted in both languages.

CONTENT OF TRAINING

The training offered covers the following main areas:

1. language enhancement;
2. agency knowledge;
3. interpreting skills.

Language enhancement is required because one or other language may be deficient in certain respects, especially where the home language and the language of education have been different. It is also intended to familiarise the students with the particular lexical registers relating to their area of work. Students work at building up their own 'termbanks' (glossaries) in both languages with the aid of language tutors.

'Agency knowledge' means knowledge about the 'agencies' or institutions for which the interpreter is required to work, and about their procedures and practice. Use is made of staff from the various agencies wherever possible, and this has had the useful side-effect of increasing user awareness of the advantages and difficulties of employing interpreters.

Training in these two areas generally took place at evening classes over a period of a year, and was followed by a two-week, full-time course in interpreting skills. However, for the course currently running in Cambridge to train interpreters for the National Health Service, which is full-time over a period of five months, it was thought preferable to begin with a two-week course in interpreting techniques, reinforced at intervals throughout the course, since students were likely to be called upon to act as interpreters within the hospital while still training, and it was felt that good habits should be inculcated from the outset.

INTERPRETING SKILLS

Students are trained to work in both consecutive and whispered simultaneous modes, and to know which is more appropriate in a given situation. Full-blown simultaneous involving the use of sound systems is not generally encountered in the world of community interpreting. Certain situations may require consecutive in one direction, but whispering in the other, e.g. at a school parents' evening with a single non-English speaking parent present it would be quite appropriate for the interpreter to whisper for the parent, but should the parent ask a question, it would require to be interpreted in consecutive. But the formalities of court procedure, for example, may require all interpreting to be consecutive even when whispering would be a sensible option.

Students are trained to take notes when working in consecutive. However, since the passages to be interpreted do not often exceed a few sentences in length, their note-taking technique does not require to be as sophisticated as that of conference interpreters. Notes are intended as an aid to remembering what has been said, not as a reliable record in themselves. No standardised system of note-taking is taught, but students are encouraged to devise their own system of mnemonics, since what is meaningful to one person may be quite unhelpful to another. Advice is, however, offered on how to organise information in note form, and suggestions may be made for symbols in particular instances.

The bulk of the training in interpreting skills is done by the use of role play. In the most successful exercises, representatives of the service agencies have acted as themselves in scenarios which they have mapped out, based on typical examples from their casework. In some cases language tutors have played the part of the 'client', in others this has been done by other students. In all cases both the language tutors and the interpreter trainer observe and make comments, either in the course of the role play, where appropriate, or at the end. The overriding criterion must be whether the message has been correctly relayed via the interpreter.

Attention is also paid to the 'ethics' of interpreting in a community environment. By this is meant not just such fundamental issues as confidentiality and strict impartiality, but also the whole business of adopting a professional approach to the job. This may involve considerations such as tidiness and punctuality, but also covers the need to ensure that the right conditions are met to enable the interpreter to work accurately and confidently. The interpreter must know how to introduce himself or herself to both parties, when and how to interrupt proceedings if explanations are required, and when to refuse an assignment, if for example one of the parties speaks an unfamiliar dialect.

It may seem difficult to believe that such a complicated package of skills can be imparted in the space of a fortnight, but the experience of the courses run thus far is that, given the proper groundwork in terms of language and background knowledge, satisfactory results can be achieved.

FUTURE DEVELOPMENTS

The present Community Interpreting Project is nearing an end, and the question that naturally arises is, where do we go from here? The ideal scenario would be for autonomous courses to be set up around the country, drawing on the experience of the project and presenting candidates for the Certificate examination. A few centres have shown interest in doing this, and some existing schemes for training community interpreters have expressed interest in becoming associated with the project, but the two obstacles to offering the Certificate on a generalised basis are (a) money, and (b) the availability of qualified trainers. The Nuffield Foundation, which has generously financed the project to date, cannot be expected to go on doing so indefinitely, and so one must look to other potential sources of assistance, whether those may be local or national government, or indeed the EEC training budget. A course to train trainers to run future courses is urgently needed if any further progress is to be made, and this subject is receiving active consideration at present.

CONCLUSION

The need for properly trained and certificated community interpreters is becoming increasingly recognised. It is possible to train suitable candidates to an acceptable standard along the lines adopted by the Community Inter-preting Project, using techniques originally developed for training conference interpreters. However, any further development will depend on the availa-bility of both adequate funding and trained personnel to run courses. Without these the current project will remain an interesting, successful, but ultimately unfruitful exercise.

On-the-job training of junior translators

Heinrich Allissat

Fried. Krupp GmbH, Essen, West Germany

The economic situation industry is facing today leaves little latitude for in-house training of junior translators. Employers expect newly recruited staff to be able to carry a full workload almost immediately.

Concurrent translation as practised at Krupp headquarters in Essen, and defined as embracing all the activities involved in completing an extensive text in camera copy at the same time as the German version, makes teamwork imperative. Experience has shown that as member of a team the junior translator gains self-confidence and self-discipline. Assigned initially to the collating function, junior translators quickly acquire the background knowledge they need such as corporate structure, organisational hierarchy and company history and become familiar with technical terms in context.

At last year's ITI conference Dr Sykes emphasised the need for vigilance in maintaining the standards of our profession. Of course, the future of the profession is in the hands of the young people now entering it. They will be the ones who will have to get to grips with the increasingly complex world of translation. We must ensure that on entering industry they are not left to pick up the job as best they can. They have to be pointed in the right direction.

Over the past twelve years or so the Krupp translation department at Group Headquarters has had a steady influx of young graduates eager to make the grade as translators. I am therefore pleased to have been given an opportunity of presenting an outline of the experience we have gained at Krupp in the training of young talent in an environment of 'concurrent' translation. I shall explain what we mean by concurrent translation later.

CURRENT SITUATION

The economic situation industry is facing today leaves little latitude for in-house training of junior translators. Employers expect newly recruited staff to be able to carry a full workload almost immediately. This means that we have to find new ways of helping the beginner gain a foothold at the start of his career.

You note I say 'his'. I shall throughout this paper apply the legal 'he' form to avoid having to keep saying 'he or she' and 'his or her'. I trust that this will not lead to my being branded as sexist.

BACKGROUND

The translation service at Krupp headquarters in Essen was established in 1952. From the very beginning we adhered to one basic principle: all translations are subjected to strict revision before they leave the department. For each language pair handled we had at least one native speaker. The English group varied in strength between eight and ten translators over the years, with one British native speaker and, temporarily, one American. When I took charge of the department twelve years ago we were faced with the problem of having to recruit young talent to replace those of my colleagues who had reached or were not far off retirement age.

THE CHOICE

The question was whether we should continue along the traditional lines with German native speakers making up the majority of the English section or whether to reverse the arrangement. The decision was not easy to take. For one thing staff turnover in the department was – and still is – minimal. If we decided to use the reverse arrangement with young Britons making up the majority of the English section, we were running the risk of recruiting people who might, after a few years, no longer be able to distinguish between a Germanism and proper English. Also, there was the question of whether young English people would want to live in the Ruhr for many years of their life. The workload of the department finally turned out to be the decisive factor. More than 90 per cent of the orders we receive are for translation from German into English, with texts for publication accounting for about 80 per cent. So there was actually no choice but to recruit young British talent if we wanted to reduce the amount of revision required before a text could be released for publication, maintain and improve our linguistic standards and operate cost-efficiently. One more thing: the trend in German industry is to encourage engineers and salesmen to improve and make active use of their knowledge of English in their work and so the number of people having a satisfactory command of English is rising. This means that most of our clients are well able to judge the quality of an English translation. So recognition of a job well done is increasing, as is the amount of criticism, whether justified or not, a translator is exposed to. If the translator is of British nationality and, on top of this, has an academic background, it is easier for the occasional sceptical client to be persuaded that the version rendered is indeed idiomatically correct English and fully reflects the meaning of the German text. Let me illustrate the problem by referring to a very interesting linguistic field – association football. It takes a lot of persuasion to make a German believe that to 'make a goal' in English means to 'provide the telling pass' and not to 'score a goal' as the literal translation into German would suggest. It's the same with 'goal kick', which in English means to boot the ball from the goal area into play and is not a shot at goal. This goes to show that knowledge of a foreign language is commendable only if the knower knows what's what and not if he merely believes what's what.

WHAT IS 'CONCURRENT' TRANSLATION?

Earlier I said that we train our young people in an environment of concurrent translation. Perhaps before I start to describe how on-the-job training works in our department I should explain what we mean by 'concurrent translation'. From your own practice you are well aware that any order placed with a translator is invariably extremely urgent. People who are quite used to accepting delivery times of weeks and months for standard industry products behave quite differently when they come near a translator's 'surgery'. They expect him and his services to be instantly available and are always quite surprised to hear that the queue is pretty long. Still, in most cases they are indeed in urgent need of help and translators have to find a way to keep everybody happy.

In our efforts to fill several orders at the same time or to complete a lengthy text by the specified 'impossible' deadline, we developed a new approach to the way we organise our work. We gave this procedure the name 'concurrent translation' – 'zeitgleiches übersetzen'. Its application meant that we had to persuade our clients to let us have their texts in draft form before completion of the final version. We convinced them that adaptation of our English draft to the final version would take little time, that we would gain time to become familiar with the subject and do the necessary terminological research and that we would thus be able to render a thoroughly researched translation by the agreed date. We have been using this procedure successfully for many years now and apply it to the translation of all texts where it is desirable for the English version to be finished at the same time as the German original. This includes the Krupp annual report, the annual reports of several subsidiaries, reports for and minutes of meetings, the Technische Mitteilungen Krupp (an engineering digest published three times a year with contributions from different disciplines and covering the whole spectrum of Krupp activities), scientific and technical papers to be read at conferences, sales literature, etc.

We have even had cases where the English clean copy was finished quicker than the German one.

IMPACT ON ON-THE-JOB TRAINING

Adoption of the concurrent approach considerably simplified and shortened the on-the-job training process. You all know how long it used to take for a young translator to reach a stage where he could work independently. Periods of three, five and more years were usually mentioned by experienced prac-titioners. There was an additional disadvantage. The constant fight against time compelled the head of the department to assign orders to those of his staff best suited for the particular job. This meant that the more prestigious texts were assigned to the senior translators and complex technical texts to those with specialist knowledge of the subject. The novice was given the rest: letters and texts of lesser importance that did not tax his knowledge, work that involved a lot of tiresome typing, etc. And this was liable to go on for years until the 'beginner' revolted or started looking for another job. What is more, the beginner was unable to learn from his colleagues. Their experience was not handed down to him.

THE COLLATING FUNCTION

With concurrent translation all this has changed. Immediately on joining the department, the newcomer becomes a member of a team and is assigned to the collating function, transferring corrections from the paper draft on-screen, critically comparing it with the original and examining it for completeness, correctness of numerical data, spelling of names, uniformity in the use of abbreviations, units of measurement, etc. The collator copies graphs and tables, glues captions, legends and words in the right places and is thus responsible for final quality control and presentation.

This immediate involvement in urgent and important translation jobs imparts self-discipline and self-confidence. In performing the collating func-tion the junior translator becomes acquainted with technical terms and concepts and their equivalents. Unfamiliar words suddenly take on meaning because they appear in context. And since the human mind functions by association, newly acquired vocabulary is added to the passive memory to stay there until needed. So our approach protects the beginner from what begin-ners in their despair do far too often: resorting as the first option to bilingual dictionaries. Signs of excessive use of such dictionaries always indicate that novices are about. Dictionaries are needed, of course, but more as a memory jogger, as an aid to finding information that can subsequently be verified in a monolingual manual or reference book.

Our experience has shown that newly recruited graduates assigned to the collating function quickly acquire the background knowledge they ultimately need to perform well as translators. By background knowledge I mean corporate structure, organisational hierarchy, the history of the company, not detailed knowledge of a machine design or operation. Knowledge of this kind is, of course, best acquired in the actual translation process. The beginner learns how to handle complex German sentences and how to make the leap from German linguistic structure to English that reads like English. He learns to appreciate the principle a translator working from German into English should be aware of: 'Subject first, and everything unfurls!'

Our principle of rigorous revision is also very important here. The beginner's work is checked by a senior translator. They then go through the text together. This gives the senior translator the opportunity to point out any pitfalls in the German text which might not have been properly overcome in the English version and gives the junior translator the opportunity to ask questions and learn from his senior colleague's experience.

We believe that this approach to on-the-job training helps to prevent the frustration and lack of recognition which beginners in a large organisation are liable to suffer. As members of a team they are not exposed to situations where they are overcome by helplessness and lost in a sea of words they do not understand. They are not left open to unjust or unjustified criticism. And so they become professionals, aware that a word processor is simply an extension of the quill pen, that translation will benefit from expert revision, and that teamwork is a must if client needs are to be met. Eagerness to play a different role in the team, to get away from the collating function and to become involved in the translation work proper, soon makes itself felt. And this, ultimately, is the objective of such on-the-job training. The transition from fledgling to full-fledged translator is, of course, a gradual but never a frustrating process.

AN EXAMPLE OF CONCURRENT REVISION

Let me mention the Krupp annual report as an example of concurrent translation. The completion dates for the German and English versions of this report are fully detailed in a tight schedule. The team assigned to its translation comprises five people, two senior translators – one who dictates the business review section, the other who works on the notes to the financial statements. A typist keyboards the dictated rough versions, and two junior translators take over standard passages from the previous year's report, make the requisite changes, prepare legends for charts, graphs and tables and translate captions. They also incorporate any incoming changes made to the German version and do a printout. The two senior translators then swop hats, each checking the part of the report translated by the other. All the changes made are entered by the junior translators on-screen and another printout is made. This is read and polished up by the two senior translators. Their changes and any additional ones meanwhile received from the client are incorporated in the body of the text by the collators. As soon as the final German version is available, a thorough check is made to ensure that both versions are indeed identical in content.

So we can see that concurrent translation not only enables us to meet customer needs but also has a spin-off in the on-the-job training of newcomers to the profession. The young translator becomes a member of a team and is involved in important jobs right from the outset. Whatever he translates himself is, of course, checked by a revisor. But revision now assumes a different role in the eyes of the novice: it is not directed at him personally, nor aimed at revealing his shortcomings, his lack of knowledge. The beginner has seen how thoroughly the senior translators mutually revise their texts, how soberly they discuss their suggestions, and how thorough they are in their search for the right phrases and technical terms. So revision loses its emotional dynamite. Its sole aim – quality – is fully evident.

COST AWARENESS

There is a further spin-off on the cost side. The practice of charging the cost of a translation direct to the account of the client exposes in-house translators to market conditions. They are expected to submit cost estimates, commit themselves to tight deadlines and quote a competitive price. What they cannot do is to refuse to accept a translation job because their order book is filled with jobs which are far more profitable and easier to do. They thus find themselves in a dilemma: they are required to ensure full cost coverage but cannot do their work selectively with emphasis on revenue. This unsatisfactory situation induced us to abandon the practice of charging translation costs per line of translated text which we had introduced in the 1960s. Our rates had reached a level where comparison with those offered on the market, chiefly by bureaus, was bound to lead to a negative attitude on the part of our clientele. So in January 1986 we adopted an hourly rate similar to the rates charged for services rendered by engineers, draughtsmen, industrial designers, EDP programmers, patent attorneys, etc. This was a bold step to take but I can assure you that it was attended with success. Because the junior translators are properly integrated in the team right from the start they soon become aware of the need to think in cost terms. Every hour of work is billed. So time must be spent productively and cost-efficiently.

EQUIPMENT

The concurrent approach, of course, requires appropriate office equipment. Each of our translators is equipped with a stand-alone word processor with two disc drives, a memory typewriter with two disc drives, and a dictating machine. The memory typewriters and word processors are compatible via a converting station and the translators are fully acquainted with three different operating systems. One of the word processors is connected to the teletex system of the German PTT. We have three letter-quality printers. The first thing the newcomer learns is how to handle all this equipment. This again is an experience that adds to his self-confidence.

Newspapers and journals to which we subscribe in order to keep abreast of developments in the areas of interest to us include *The Times*, *The Economist*, *Wall Street Journal*, *Harvard Business Review*, *Mechanical Engineering*, *Cutting Tool Engineering* and *The Steel Times*.

CONCLUSION

To sum up then: our approach to on-the-job training is based on two important aspects of our work – concurrent translation and the billing of work at an hourly rate. We have found that by pursuing this approach we are best equipped to provide effective training while meeting economic constraints. From day one the newcomer to the business is fulfilling an important role in the team and, perhaps more important, his active and passive memory is accumulating the knowledge needed for a satisfying career.

Session 3: Report of discussion

Rapporteur: Jane Taylor, University of Manchester, UK

Hugh Keith, as Chairman, thanked all three speakers for their valuable contributions: although a detailed discussion might mean that the session would overrun slightly, he could see such signs of interest and enthusiasm in the audience that he proposed to prolong it. He opened the floor to questions and comments, which ranged over all stages in the fledgling translator's development.

PRE-UNIVERSITY LEVEL

Barbara Snell was particularly eager to know what opportunities existed for young people to have some work-experience before committing themselves to a demanding four-year course: this might enhance their determination, and make them more aware of the real needs their course was designed to meet. There were nods around the hall; clearly this had struck a chord. Michael Croft agreed that this might be more than worthwhile, but while many undergraduate courses recognise the value of work-experience by organising placements for their undergraduates, no formal provision existed for this at pre-university level; on an ad hoc basis, of course, some future students might be able to make their own arrangements. John Graham was able to tell members that West Germany had instituted just such a scheme: grammar school students were able to spend a week in each of a number of different professional environments to explore the nature of the work involved before committing themselves to a course of study, and his own Department regularly accommodated six to ten pupils a year, of whom as many as five might go on to study translation and interpreting. Sally Walker warmed to the idea; fourth- and fifth-formers might well be offered work experience with her own company through careers officers or through the University of Bath.

UNDERGRADUATE LEVEL

Interestingly, less attention was given to this level than to the others. David Denby of the National Institute of Higher Education, Dublin, however, in a brief intervention, wanted to emphasise that two facets of training needed distinguishing at the undergraduate level. Students' skills needed developing and enhancing in two quite separate areas: language competence and translation skills. It was important that both should be allowed equal weight. Hugh Keith agreed, but pointed out that as written language skills in particular might receive less attention in schools under the new General Certificate of Secondary Education system, educational institutions would need to spend more and more time on enhancing more elementary language skills.

POST-GRADUATE LEVEL

Several speakers underlined the urgent need for more post-graduate provision in the way of short courses or part-time qualifications. Melanie Dean, seconded by Claude Fleurent, was disappointed that there was little or no provision in London or the Home Counties for the young translator in full-time employment to work for a part-time M.A./M.Sc. in interpreting/translating (on the model of that in the University of Salford), or to follow short, tailor-made courses. Jamila Bernat, herself a community interpreter, was eager that the sort of short-course training described by Alastair Scouller should be extended; generously, she expressed herself willing to contribute her own time to such training. But neither Michael Croft nor Alastair Scouller could be optimistic: such requests come up against the hard facts of further and continuing education funding. It was increasingly necessary to make part-time courses and short courses commercially viable, and this had serious implications for costing and for size of groups: part-time courses needed large numbers to be financially viable. And even where short courses for specific needs did exist, and where efforts were being made to respond to stated demand, as at PCL, there were worrying funding problems.

Given this depressing situation, Mary Cotton made the suggestion that perhaps retired translators and interpreters, or those with some spare time, might be able, given the premises, to offer some training to the young translator. Michael Croft was impressed by the generosity of this suggestion: already, at the University of Bath, practising translators give their time free to working with trainees. But a voluntary system of this sort could be no substitute for properly funded courses.

It was pleasant to turn to the promising and successful concurrent training scheme run by Krupp in West Germany. To a question from Raymond Hooper, Heinrich Allissat agreed that such a system had significantly reduced the time needed for the young post-graduate to become a useful translator. Patricia Crampton suggested a further refinement: given that native language proficiency can often slip in a second-language environment, and that Krupp employs U.K. graduates, had any thought been given to organising 'refresher' exchange schemes with U.K. companies? Heinrich Allissat was aware of the danger, but there were at present no plans of this sort.

The equally successful community interpreting course described by Alistair Scouller elicited the enthusiastic support of Claire Kahtan. What, she wondered, where the linguistic and educational qualifications for enrolment on courses? Alistair Scouller replied that he and his team-members would look for high proficiency in both languages involved, perhaps using the Institute of

Linguists' Bilingual Skills certificate as a concrete point of reference; although the interpreters would generally not hold degrees in either of the two languages involved, they would normally have an educational standard equivalent to degree-level, and at the admission stage they would be interviewed in both languages, and asked to produce written translations.

Session 4: Theory and practice of translation

Chaired by Ewald Osers

Technical and literary translation: a unifying view

Danica Seleskovitch

Université Paris III (ESIT), France

The necessity of matching precise technical terms in two languages is often considered to be the main if not the only difficulty of technical translation. It will be shown on the basis of an example that technical translation requires in addition to correct wording a sound understanding of the things meant by a text; cognitive complements play as important a role in technical translation as in other kinds of translation.

The difficulties of literary translation are often seen not in the transfer of meaning from one language to another but in the rendering of the intricacies of an author's language. A French translation of a short English poem will show the extent to which cognitive complements contribute to solving language problems in literary translation.

Both in technical and in literary translation sense shapes the expressiveness of the target language.

At first sight there seems to be a vast difference between technical and literary translation. The individuals who work on technical texts are rarely the same as those who translate works of literature. This partition is clearly brought out within the international organisation, FIT, where literary and technical translators meet in two separate committees.

My purpose here is to show that, separate as they may be in the practice of individual translators, literary and technical translations have one aspect in common: they deal with texts, not only with languages. Text versus language is the main difference between human and machine translation, for instance, or translation in language teaching classes.

The difference is easy to understand: translating texts requires in addition to a competence in languages an unquestionable knowledge of the world. That world might be a world of fiction as in most literary texts or the real world of technology, but in both cases, to make good translating of texts possible, world knowledge has to be added to a competence in languages.

It is fitting, I think, since this conference is held at Russell Square, to mention a polemical issue raised by Roman Jakobson with Bertrand Russell who had stated that:

> No-one can understand the word cheese unless he has a non-linguistic acquaintance with cheese.

To that statement R. Jakobson replied [1]:

> If . . . we . . . place our 'emphasis upon the linguistic aspects of traditional philosophical problems', (as Russell himself said) then we are obliged to state that no one can understand the word cheese unless he has an acquaintance with the meaning assigned to this word in the lexical code of English.

The controversy is of interest to translators as it shows the two levels at which translating is apt to be performed: *language level*, as in language teaching or in machine translation, or in the setting up of bilingual dictionaries, and *text level* as with human translating or interpreting.

Let us take two examples chosen from technical and literary sources and see the differences involved in translating according to whether the text is dealt with at language level or at text level.

TECHNICAL TEXTS

Here is an excerpt from a technical report of the Environment and Consumer Protection Service of the EEC in Brussels, reproduced in the review *Engineering* and used in a translation class by one of our colleagues at ESIT, Dr C. Durieux [2] whose book on the pedagogy of technical translation will soon be published:

> Cadmium is a dangerous pollutant in addition to being an expensive metal and on both scores the elimination of cadmium emissions to the environment is important. The means of achieving this and of recovering cadmium for re-use are reviewed in a report from the Environment and Consumer Protection Service of the EEC.
>
> The report examines methods for removing cadmium from waste water and exhaust air and for reducing the cadmium content of materials disposed of in dumps. The efficiency of existing recovery methods and new opportunities for reducing environmental pollution by cadmium are also examined. The economic consequences of reducing cadmium emission limits are assessed.

The last sentence of this text was misinterpreted by a number of students at ESIT. They produced a number of translations implying that *limitations* on cadmium emissions were to be reduced, which would mean that a larger, not a smaller quantity of cadmium would be released. Apparently those students did not take into account the co-text which indicates that cadmium is a pollutant so that cadmium emissions to the environment should be reduced, and were too much concerned with the rendering of 'limits'; to make it sound French, they wrote *'abaisser le seuil'* in a number of cases.

Based on the small knowledge brought by the co-text a correct translation of that sentence would read in French:

On évalue les conséquences économiques qu'aurait une réduction des niveaux d'émission du cadmium.

LITERARY TEXTS

Let us take our second example, a short poem by the British poet Siegfried Sassoon:

> Was ever immolation so belied
> As these intolerably nameless names?

Those two lines, read in the absence of further information, offer only their language meanings; they are lifeless. Any attempt at translating them would be devoid of poetry:

> *Jamais immolation fut-elle aussi désavouée*
> *Que par ces noms intolérablement anonymes?*

In order to understand the sense of these two English lines, to feel their emotional impact and to be able to transmit it in French, a translator has to draw on knowledge that is not verbalised but assumed. Sassoon fought in the First World War and took part in the murderous battles of Ypres, where he was seriously wounded. At these battles, losses in life of British and Empire troops ran into tens of thousands, as Allied offensives and German counter-offensives followed each other week after week.

After the war, the Imperial War Graves Commission had a memorial built on the site of that tragedy: the Menin Gate, named after a village that was stormed many times. On it are engraved the names of the 55,000 men lost in battle whose corpses were never identified.

Now we understand Sassoon's words, 'Was ever immolation so belied/As these intolerably nameless names?', now we sympathise with his feelings as he stood looking at the Menin Gate and we are in a position to make another try at rendering it in French:

> *Horreur insoutenable de ces noms sans nombre*
> *Abominable, absurde immolation.*

This translation of Sassoon's poem was arrived at in one of our classes at ESIT; it is but one translation out of many possible ones; it could probably be improved upon; one thing however is certain: in this case as in all cases non-linguistic information had to be added to language competence to arouse feelings and to produce a translation that seeks to have the same impact on the French reader as Sassoon had on an English reader.

Language meanings by themselves do not provide enough information for the translation of texts. Extra-linguistic knowledge has to be available to enable the translator to transmit the factual content of technical texts and the factual and emotional content of literary texts. Only when language meanings combine with extra-linguistic information does sense arise, i.e. does the translator understand the full meaning of the text and is therefore able to convey it in another language.

TRANSLATING VERSUS TRANSCODING, SENSE VERSUS MEANING

Let me enlarge on the contention that no successful translation can be made on the basis of language alone.

Language in isolation, *langue* as defined by Saussure, is an abstract system or code. The operation which puts down language corresponding to another language, should be called transcoding since it deals only with the language codes, with meanings codified in each language. In that case, words such as 'limits' in our technical text or 'belie' in Sassoon's poem would have to be weighed against their French correspondences. (E) 'Limits' might correspond to (F) *'limites'*, *'frontières'*, *'ligne de démarcation'*, *'périmètre'*, *'périphérie'*, etc.; none of these, however, would be suitable in the sentence '. . . reducing cadmium emission limits', and yet that word 'limits' could not be transcoded, i.e. translated at language level, by *'niveau'* as we did when translating at text level: (*'une réduction des niveaux d'émission du cadmium'*).

Take 'belie'; at language level we might transcode: *'désavouer'*, *'contredire'*, *'nier'*, *'fausser'*, *'pervertir'*, *'minimiser'*, etc., but in no case would transcoding enable us to write *'abominable, absurde . . .'* (*'abominable, absurde immolation'*). In both cases we established not a correspondence at language level but an equivalence at text level.

Translation at language level is *transcoding*, the products of transcoding are *correspondences*, which will never make for good translation of texts. Transcoding may produce correct entries in bilingual dictionaries, excellent comparative grammars, usable machine translations, but it cannot generate technical or literary translations that would be acceptable equivalents of the original texts such as good human translators are apt to produce.

The reason is easy to understand if we look at the difference between texts and language. Texts convey more than their language meanings; they have an author – whose personality is important for the literary translator – or at least a source, and it is not indifferent for the understanding of a technical text to know whence the information comes; texts are written at a given point in time and space that reflect a given culture; they are directed at certain types of reader, they imply a knowledge underlying words and phrases, that has to be shared. The reader, and even more so the translator, shares that knowledge and brings it to bear in his or her translation.

As I have said and written many times [3], the inadequacy of language translating of texts is due to the fact that non-linguistic encyclopaedic knowledge is ignored whereas understanding of discourses – be they written texts or oral speeches – always involves world knowledge in addition to language competence.

We call 'sense' the combination of language meanings and relevant world knowledge. Sense if found in texts, meanings in languages. In French we use the word *'sens'* as opposed to *'signification'*, in German *'Sinn'* as opposed to *'Bedeutung'*.

The language philosopher Eugenio Coseriu clearly distinguishes between the levels of language and of text; with Saussure, he speaks of *signifier* for language sounds and of *signified* for language meanings but he adds that, at text level, language sounds *and* language meanings are *signifiers*, while in a discourse it is sense (*Sinn*) which is the *signified*, i.e. that which is conveyed.

Both technical and literary translations deal with texts and the reader of texts automatically connects his reading with his or her knowledge of the world, making sense out of language. So that things or ideas referred to grow into a language-independent existence.

Our research team at ESIT calls *compléments cognitifs* (cognitive complements) the knowledge of things that changes language meanings into author's meaning or sense. Cognitive complements are of two kinds: *contexte cognitif*, i.e. the cognitive co-text and *bagage cognitif*, world knowledge. *Contexte cognitif*, cognitive co-text, is the knowledge acquired during reading that helps in understanding the further word sequences of a text. It stems from the text itself. The information supplied by the cognitive co-text enhances our interpretative ability to understand the sense of the sentences we read. *Bagage cognitif*, relevant world knowledge, also enhances our interpretative capacity and brings us away from mere recognition of semantics.

Sense is the unifying link between literary and technical translation.

It is often believed that the difficulties met in translating literary works are due to the necessity of reproducing an author's style; but style stems from sense as much as it contributes to sense; whatever the style of a written or oral utterance, as long as it is meant as a message, that style will be part of the sense to be conveyed. It will be reflected in the other language by style that is not a conversion of the original style but the expression of the translator's understanding of sense.

It is often believed that technical translation requires not much beside the matching of corresponding technical terms. It is true that part of the technical translator's work is to find the correct correspondences for individual terms but no technical text is entirely made up of technical terms unless it is purely descriptive or intended as a nomenclature. As soon as there is a reasoning behind the words, there is a sense to be understood and to be conveyed in the target language and that requires more than the knowledge of corresponding words or sentences.

Perhaps it is time for me to return to Russell Square and to conclude. Translators should unhesitatingly side with Bertrand Russell in the controversy on the linguistic or non-linguistic meaning of 'cheese'. Sense is not understood merely on the basis of our 'acquaintance with the meaning assigned to words in any lexical code' but 'on the basis of our non-linguistic acquaintance with the matter of things' as Bertrand Russell puts it.

Both practitioners and theoreticians of translation cannot but feel that in connection with translating Bertrand Russell is right and Roman Jakobson wrong.

REFERENCES

[1] JAKOBSON, R.: 'On linguistic aspects of translation', *Selected Writings II*, p. 260. Mouton, 1971.
[2] DURIEUX, C.: *Fondement didactique de la traduction technique*, to be published by Didier Erudition, Paris.
[3] SELESKOVITCH, D. and LEDERER, M.: *Interpréter pour traduire*. Didier Erudition, Paris, 1984.

The dramatic translator

Robert David MacDonald

Citizens Theatre, Glasgow

Note from the editor:

This paper was one of those lively, stimulating presentations which owe everything to spontaneity and very little to a text prepared in advance. Mr MacDonald tells me that he had no hard and fast script for his talk, just a few notes and headings. The basic theme of what he had to say is to be found in his preface to *Faust* (Oberon Books), adapted of course to suit the particular linguistic interests of the conference participants.

Scientific translation – pitfalls and problems

E. Boris Uvarov

Lexicographer and freelance translator

A brief introduction is followed by discussion of the following topics: Requirements for competent scientific translation. Dictionaries and other aids, with special reference to chemistry. Different source languages and types of texts: books, journals (cover-to-cover and individual papers); patents, in-house material. Presentation of translated texts of different types. The translator as editor. Recognition of pitfalls and problems, their causes and origins, and ways of dealing with them. International systems of nomenclature in chemistry (IUPAC), and of units and measurements in physics (SI). Nomenclature problems in chemistry, from IUPAC to acronyms and code designations.

INTRODUCTION

It is not my aim in this paper to tell fellow-translators how to do their job. Indeed, with so many excellent translators around, it would be gross impertinence on my part to do so. However, as most of us are largely self-taught, we no doubt differ widely in experience and approach, and I offer my paper as a contribution to shared experience.

It is interesting to ponder why or how we became translators; probably not in fulfilment of early ambitions. A burning wish to be a rock star, brain surgeon, snooker champion, or prime minister might be understood and even encouraged; an urge to become a translator would be more likely to lead to a visit to a psychiatrist.

My first steps into translation were taken in 1920, when at the age of ten I arrived with my parents in England from Russia after a few weeks of tuition (of doubtful value) in English. I was led to believe that all language problems can be solved with the aid of a device called a dictionary, in which the required words are given opposite their Russian equivalents. Reading, I was assured, is no problem either: each English letter has its Russian equivalent, and one merely substitutes and reads out the result. However, it did not work very well. My English schoolfellows gained a lot of pleasure from my efforts at reading, while I acquired a healthy scepticism in the use of dictionaries, which has survived to the present day.

Much of this paper, and virtually all of my translating experience, is concerned with translation of Russian scientific (mainly chemical) journals and books into English, but certain general ideas and principles are broadly valid for most European source and target languages. Those interested in translation of German and French chemical texts into English will find the knowledgeable and detailed paper by W.G. Barb [1] useful. It contains numerous specific examples of problems in translation from these languages, together with comments on patents and EEC documents. The basic message of Barb's paper is that translators of chemical material must be chemists.

REQUIREMENTS AND AIDS FOR COMPETENT TRANSLATION

I will begin with the general principle, stated so often in various forms as to be a truism, of three basic requirements which a proficient scientific translator must satisfy: (1) clear comprehension of (but not necessarily fluency in) the source language; (2) knowledge of the subject to a high level, supported by access to reliable sources of the latest information on that subject; (3) fluency in (ideally, ability to think in) the target language. I doubt whether these requirements can be usefully arranged in order of importance; failure in any one can ruin a translation. Obviously, no translator can be so proficient or so self-confident as to claim 100 per cent efficiency in each requirement; a conscientious translator must correspondingly devote more time and effort to produce an acceptable result. In other words, a translator in such a position must rely to a greater extent on published material such as dictionaries and other reference works and must learn to assess their reliability.

DICTIONARIES AND OTHER REFERENCE MATERIAL

Here I must 'declare an interest'; over many years I have been involved in various ways with several dictionaries, and it would not be proper for me to comment on the merits or faults of any particular dictionary. However, some general comments on their value as sources of information should be made. First, no printed dictionary of any developing scientific or technical subject can possibly be either up to date or complete; the speed with which new scientific terms and techniques appear greatly exceeds the speed of compilation and publication. Secondly, it is worth while to assess the reliability of any specialised dictionary by examining its antecedents and by testing its treatment of known 'difficult' terms. A dictionary of wide scope, covering several subjects, is more likely to be reliable if it is compiled, or at the very least edited, by a team of acknowledged specialists in those subjects. Verification of terms given in different dictionaries can be misleading. Consider three examples, all of Russian terms: the acronym *GOST* (*Gosudarstvennyi Obshchesoyuznyi Standart*, State All-Union Standard) is given in several dictionaries as 'All-Union State Standard' (wrong word order); '*ionit*' is the usual Russian term for ion exchanger or ion-exchange resin, but its apparent equivalent 'ionite' should never be used in that sense in English, and yet it is repeatedly given as such in dictionaries, together with the equally unacceptable 'anionite' and 'cationite'; and, finally, the Russian word '*samovar*', given repeatedly in dictionaries as 'tea urn', which it isn't. This one has been used by Our Own Correspondent in Moscow (along with the oligatory *glasnost* and *perestroika* in other contexts) in referring to Soviet leaders peering at tea leaves in their *samovars* to read the future. Those who look for tea leaves in *samovars* obviously don't know their *samovars* from their *chainiks*.

Here we have the same three demonstrable errors repeated in several dictionaries. So, what are often described as 'reliable sources' are all too often sources of perpetuated error. Finally, let us consider chemical dictionaries. Because of the astronomical number of reported chemical compounds, it is impossible in practice to include more than a tiny fraction in a dictionary of reasonable size. For translation, for example, of a research paper on chemical reactions involving compounds with complicated names the translator must identify the compounds from formulae or other information given (or implied) in the text. If these compounds have to be named, the translator must use his or her chemical knowledge to construct the names in accordance with recognised rules of chemical nomenclature, such as those of the International Union of Pure and Applied Chemistry (IUPAC). Mere transliteration is risky at best. However, help is often at hand in the form of literature references to earlier work on the same subject. The sources cited can usually be seen in a specialist library and may, with luck, be in English. Of course, the naming of chemical compounds (chemical nomenclature) is only a fraction of the translator's task; there may also be processes, scientific instruments, theories, and named reactions to be identified and converted to the target language. Here, too, reference material other than dictionaries is often essential. The most frequently used sources of information in my own collection include a large general scientific encyclopaedia [2], a chemical and technological encyclopaedia [3], a handbook of chemical engineering ('Perry') [4], IUPAC nomenclature rules, organic ('Blue Book') [5] and inorganic ('Red Book') [6], IUPAC terminology recommendations [7], and a mathematical handbook [8].

In addition to their own libraries to suit their special needs, most translators need to have access (in specialist libraries) to abstracts and annual reviews in their subject fields.

Even with the major problem of actual terminology taken care of on the lines I have suggested, the translator's troubles may be only just beginning. The reason is that all these nomenclature rules, terminology guides, etc., are fully valid only for ideal texts, free from errors and lucidly presented in the source language, using consistent symbols and units and citing identifiable literature references, but, as all translators know, such gems are rare, especially in the applied sciences. That is the *raison d'être* of this paper, which is largely an attempt to bridge the gap between the ideal and the real by examining the pitfalls and problems of scientific and technical translation.

INTERNATIONAL NOMENCLATURE AND MEASUREMENT SYSTEMS

I have already referred briefly to the IUPAC nomenclature rules for chemistry [5,6]. These rules, formulated and periodically revised by relevant commissions of the International Union of Pure and Applied Chemistry and adapted in a consistent manner for different languages, have made an enormous contribution to chemical nomenclature, while allowing retention of many well-established older names of chemical compounds. No serious translator of chemical literature can afford to disregard them.

Another aspect of scientific information is that of units of measurement, of paramount importance in all the exact sciences. Like the IUPAC nomenclature system in chemistry, the International System of units (SI units) is the recommended and widely adopted system of units and measurements in physics, chemistry, and allied disciplines. Being relative newcomers, neither is the only system in its own field. Incorrect use of SI units can lead to spectacular errors, to which I will refer in discussing pitfalls. Tables of SI units are given in a number of reference works, e.g. *Van Nostrand's scientific encyclopaedia* [2].

DIFFERENT TYPES OF TEXTS

Most of the scientific material currently being translated into English is in the form of journals, and most of those are Russian. This has been discussed in some detail by Albin Tybulewicz [9]. Cover-to-cover translation of Russian scientific and technical journals is a full-time occupation for many translators, both in Britain and in the United States, and the standard of this work is generally very high. However, there is a potential weakness in the existing system: many papers published in journals are parts of series rather than self-contained entities. Sometimes different papers in the same series are translated by different translators, and this may result in inconsistencies. Before starting to translate a journal paper, the translator would be wise to look at the 'literature cited' section to clarify this point and to proceed accordingly. Apparent problems arising in translation of journal papers can sometimes be resolved in this way. Journal translation is probably the most demanding of the different types: the subject-matter may be unexpectedly esoteric, and the style of different authors ranges from lucid to totally incomprehensible (described unofficially in certain circles as BBB – brain-boggling bull).

Translation of literature citations, especially in Russian journals citing non-Russian publications, can be very time-consuming. I will have more to say about this later.

Books (monographs) are, in my view, the most rewarding of the different types of texts. With the subject defined, background material is easier to assemble; the scope is narrower, and the written style is more consistent than in a journal. Unless the subject is particularly obscure or new, it is often possible to find a recent work on that subject in the target language; this is very helpful for getting the specialist terminology right.

Patents are highly specialised documents; for legal reasons, extra care is needed for their translation. This has been discussed in some detail by Barb [1].

PITFALLS AND PROBLEMS

The trouble with pitfalls is that you don't recognise them until you are in one (that is what pitfalls were invented for), and with problems, that when you meet one you don't know what to do.

Let us first consider pitfalls, or traps for the unwary. I must apologise here to readers who are not familiar with Russian: many pitfalls are specific to one language, and within the scope of this paper that language must be Russian. They usually originate from undetected errors or ambiguities in the source text, or from subtle changes of meaning of words adopted from one language into the other. Some are well known, like the Russian noun '*intelligent*', others, in the scientific and technical field, ought to be spotted by the careful translator. One such is the word '*produkt*', which in Russian often means merely 'substance', not necessarily the product of some specific operation or reaction. '*Sintez*' (synthesis) is often used by Russian authors to denote 'preparation' and not in the strict meaning of the word 'synthesis' in chemistry. The word '*reagent*' is used in Russian in a broader sense than 'reagent' in English, where it normally denotes a specific agent, e.g. in analysis (silver nitrate is a reagent for chloride), while in Russian it means any reacting substance, the preferable English term being 'reactant'.

The English word 'concentration' has two different meanings in the scientific sense: the relative content of a component, and the process of increasing that content, i.e. concentrating. The use of the latter as a noun or gerund in English sometimes leads to awkward sentence construction, but the Russians have the advantage of two distinct nouns derived from the same root: '*kontsentratsiya*' for the relative content and '*kontsentrirovanie*' for the process. Another example of manufacture of an additional Russian word from an English root form is the use of the words '*ekstraktsiya*' and '*ekstra-girovanie*' for what appears to be 'extraction' in both cases. In reality, the former means liquid extraction (solvent extraction) from one liquid into another, while the other is leaching (by a liquid out of a solid).

The Russian word '*vosstanovlenie*' means 'reduction' in the chemical sense. However, in ordinary speech it also means 'restoration' (to an original state). This leads to a pitfall in the chemistry of industrial manufacture of phosphorus. Phosphorus is obtained by chemical reduction of phosphate ores; the corresponding Russian expression is *'vosstanovlenie fosfora'*, which an unwary translator might render as 'reduction of phosphorus', but is in fact reduction of the ore *to* phosphorus, or production of phosphorus by reduction from the ore.

Persistent dictionary errors qualify as pitfalls. Some of them can be attributed to indiscriminate use of different nomenclature systems, and they should be detected and avoided by competent chemists.

Incorrect use of SI units is a rich source of pitfalls, especially when the SI symbols are transliterated into Russian. In the Russian alphabet the capital and lower case (M or m) are very similar, differing noticeably only in size; but in SI units the prefix M stands for mega (multiply by a million), whereas the lower case m stands for milli (one thousandth, as in millimetre). When these two symbols are confused in the original text, as occasionally happens, the size of the resultant error is truly astronomical. Numerical data, especially when presented in the 'scientific' system of notation (in powers of ten), should always be checked to see if they make sense. In a recent publication the duration of a corrosion test was given as a multiple of 10^9 seconds, suggesting that the test was started at some time during the reign of Peter the Great. Excessive zeal in the use of SI units can also be a needless nuisance: in another paper the length of an industrial trial was given as $3.1536 \cdot 10^7$ seconds, which is an excessively erudite way of saying one year.

We now come to problems. I often envy the preacher cited by Edward Cartmell [10] in his excellent monograph on crystal chemistry: 'Here, O Lord, we come to a difficulty, and having looked it boldly in the face, we pass on.' This may be forgiven in Heaven to theologians, but not down here to translators. There is, of course, no limit to the number of terms, expressions, and concepts that can bring the translator to a grinding halt. One of the commonest is the choice of nomenclature in chemistry. Pedantically, the best (some may even argue, the only) choice is the IUPAC system but, depending on the scientific level and the purpose of a particular text, there are several options: trivial or common names, chemically valid but deviating from the IUPAC system; trade names, including registered trademarks; acronyms and abbreviations (e.g. PVC); pharmaceutical names; alternative names, such as identical dyes marketed by different firms; code designations, etc. A worthwhile discussion of this problem would need much more space than I am allowed here, and I can only suggest that the scientific level and general tone of the translation should be consistent with the original text.

A recurrent problem is that of subscripts and superscripts in empirical mathematical formulae, very common in chemical kinetics and chemical engineering. These are usually ad hoc symbols, whose meanings should be explained by the original authors, and translated accordingly. However, this often leads to trouble: two words having different initial letters in Russian may have the same initial in English. Where the number of such symbols is large, the Russian authors have the advantage of three different alphabets (Russian, Roman, and Greek) to choose from, whereas the translator has only two. To make matters worse, the original authors do not always explain their notation.

When the subject-matter of the source text has been clearly understood and the equivalent English terminology has been found, the translator must express the material in lucid English, avoiding foreign forms of style and sentence construction, such as reversal of normal English word order ('backward ran the sentences until boggled the mind'), long chains of adjectival clauses, excessive use of abstract nouns, and so on. Pleonastic writing should be pruned ruthlessly: expressions such as 'analysis of our experimental data permits us to draw the conclusion that' can be changed to 'our results show that' without significant loss of meaning.

Earlier in this paper I said that I was unwilling to discuss the merits of individual dictionaries. I should have added 'of the conventional type.' Zimmerman's *Russian–English translator's dictionary* [11] is described better by its subtitle, 'A guide to scientific and technical usage.' It does not aim to give the meanings of individual words but is an excellent guide to correct phraseology and is very helpful in cases where the meaning of a Russian expression is understood but difficult to express in good idiomatic English, and so it should be especially useful to translators with less than perfect knowledge of English. I have found it very helpful in dealing with sentences involving such general-purpose Russian prepositions as *po* and *pri*. Translators of Russian will know what I mean.

As I mentioned earlier, identifying literature citations in Russian publications and putting them into the correct original form is a serious and tedious problem. In some Russian journals the titles of books of Western origin are translated, sometimes loosely, into Russian and the authors' names are transliterated into Russian. Occasionally the Russian guesses at the correct pronunciation (and here we must sympathise with their translators) are hard to identify, and it is not at all easy to get the whole reference back into the original form. However, it is imperative to do so when translating for publication; failure to identify important Western books and authors reflects badly on the translator. Generally the easiest route to identification of scientific references is through the author index of an appropriate abstracting journal, such as *Chemical Abstracts*.

THE TRANSLATOR AS EDITOR

The extent to which the translator should edit the original text is a controversial matter. All will agree that obvious misprints should be corrected by the translator; but beyond that, what? At the other extreme, should the translator convert physical units and quantities to SI units, or chemical nomenclature to the IUPAC system?

How far should the translator go in changing the wording or sentence construction in order to improve clarity? My own feeling is that the translation should be as close as possible to the scientific level of the original; if the author writes at a high scientific level and uses SI units, or IUPAC nomenclature, or both, this should be adhered to strictly in the translation and any apparently inadvertent deviations should be amended. However, if, for example, a chemical paper deals with an industrial process and uses generally accepted trivial names rather than IUPAC terms, e.g. nitrocellulose rather than cellulose nitrate, the translation should follow suit. In general, the translator should adhere to the author's intentions and terminology even if he or she disagrees with them. In particular, the translator must be absolutely certain before correcting any apparent error, and even then should point it out to the eventual reader if circumstances permit. In other words, the translator is the author's loyal agent, not mentor. Equally, his or her duty to the reader is to present an accurate and lucid version of the original text.

CONCLUSION

From a glance over the state of translation over the past half-century, one fact is clear: Gresham's law (bad money drives out the good) does not apply to translation. In the first half of this century most translation of Russian literature ranged from mediocre to atrocious and the small amount of translated Russian scientific material was of dubious merit; now there is no doubt that good translation has driven out the bad.

I would like to end on a Presidential note, by quoting a Russian proverb, particularly appropriate to translation; it is a more forceful version of 'live and learn': '*Vek zhivi, vek uchis*'.

REFERENCES

[1]   BARB, W. G. The translation of German and French chemical texts into English, *Chemistry in Britain*, 17, 12, December 1981, 566-572.
[2]   CONSIDINE, D. M. and CONSIDINE G. D. (eds.), *Van Nostrand's scientific encyclopedia*, 6th ed. New York: Van Nostrand Reinhold, 1976.
[3]   CONSIDINE, D. M. (editor-in-chief), *Chemical and process technology encyclopedia*. New York: McGraw-Hill, 1974.
[4]   PERRY, R. H. and GREEN, D. (editorial directors), *Perry's chemical engineers' handbook*, 6th ed. New York: McGraw-Hill, 1984.
[5]   International Union of Pure and Applied Chemistry (IUPAC), *Nomenclature of organic chemistry*, sections A,B,C,D,E,F and H. Oxford: Pergamon, 1979.
[6]   International Union of Pure and Applied Chemistry (IUPAC), *Nomenclature of inorganic chemistry*, 2nd ed. London: Butterworths, 1970.
[7]   GOLD, V. *et al.*, *Compendium of chemical terminology, IUPAC recommendations*. Oxford: Blackwell Scientific Publications, 1987.
[8]   KORN, G. A. and KORN, T. M., *Mathematical handbook for scientists and engineers*, 2nd ed. New York: McGraw-Hill, 1968.

[9]   TYBULEWICZ, A., Appendix A, cover-to-cover and selective journal translations, in: *The translator's handbook*, edited by C. Picken, pp. 241-242, London: Aslib, 1983.

[10]   CARTMELL, E., *Principles of crystal chemistry*, p. 15. London: Royal Institute of Chemistry, 1971.

[11]   ZIMMERMAN, M., *Russian–English translator's dictionary: a guide to scientific and technical usage*, 2nd ed. New York: Wiley & Sons, 1984.

Session 4: Report of discussion

Rapporteur: Ros Schwartz, freelance translator

THE IMPLICIT BECOMES EXPLICIT

David Snelling from the University of Trieste asked Professor Seleskovitch to comment on her choice of words used to translate the Sassoon poem cited as an example in her paper. He pointed out that the words '*horreur*', '*abominable*' and '*absurde*' were much stronger than 'belie' and 'intolerably'. Did this mean that in the translation process, that which is implicit in the source text becomes explicit in the target language?

Professor Seleskovitch replied that one should not concentrate on the meaning of each word. The poet wishes the poem to be understood with the intellect and to make an impact on the reader's emotions. If that impact is achieved in the target language, then the translator has been faithful. Choices rightly or wrongly have to be made but based on the overall view of the meaning, not on the single term in isolation.

TEACHING TECHNIQUES

Dragana Trandafilovic Alvarez, a freelance translator involved in training in Yugoslavia, asked Professor Seleskovitch how one teaches students to translate ambiguous, convoluted sentences correctly. The answer was very simply to read the text; turn it over and then say what was meant. Remember the purpose of the text, not the individual words. Whatever the actual wording used, students understand the sense. Once the meaning has been elucidated, one should return to the text and find the best word in the target language to convey the sense.

Jane Taylor from the University of Manchester pointed out that Professor Seleskovitch's approach demanded great fluency and flexibility in the use of the mother-tongue. She asked what ESIT did about mother-tongue enhancement. The professor replied that mother-tongue flexibility was determined by comprehensive testing at entrance level. Nothing was done subsequently to improve it. They also require perfect command of a foreign language – which can never be true.

VERSE IS WORSE – OR IS IT?

John Hudson, ex-Diplomatic Service, asked Robert Macdonald what he thought of the recent translation of Racine produced by Jonathan Miller and how Victor Hugo could write about verse as 'optical thought'.

Mr Macdonald found Miller's Racine dreadful and said that audiences thought it was funny. Racine is a serious writer – there is not one joke in his entire works – so if the translation makes people laugh, then it has failed. He went on to discuss the difficulty of getting verse accepted in the English theatre. All rhyming text sounds like TV jingles on the stage, which is distressing. As for Hugo, he did not write for the theatre. The definition cited is from the preface to *Cromwell*, his first play. He was first and foremost a poet, and Robert Macdonald agreed with his definition up to a point. For example, in a play like *Faust*, the form changes constantly and the look of the page dictates what the author is driving at. He felt that if a distinguished author chooses a certain metre it is absolutely up to the translator to follow, whether he or she is sympathetic or not.

Gery Bramall mentioned the difficulty of translating opera libretti and, more importantly in her opinion, poems precisely as opposed to poetically, especially if the sense is obscure and the language archaic. Existing translations often vary considerably. Robert Macdonald agreed that opera posed very specific problems because the singers wish to display their voices to their best advantage and may object to certain vowels being used in certain places. The translator has to be aware of this although you can't kowtow endlessly. One has to be aware of the demands of the music – for example, in Strauss's *Der Rosenkavalier*, when Octavian presents the bride with a rose, in the German there is a series of tight vowels in a very short time, and this is done for a specific purpose. As for Lady Bramall's point about poetry, it is virtually impossible for two translators to come up with the same translation.

A QUESTION OF FORM

At this point, Ewald Osers intervened from the chair to question the claim that Alexandrines must be translated into Alexandrines. Although a translation in blank verse is unacceptable, is there a satisfactory form of verse that will produce a similar effect as the Alexandrine did on the French two hundred years ago? He felt that certain forms are alien to the English-speaking theatre-goer and it is therefore legitimate for the translator to question, as it is with poetry, the importance of the formal element. It is purely a traditional garment, used out of habit, or does it convey an emotional message? Perhaps the translator should choose the appropriate form to convey the same emotional charge to the theatre-goer.

Robert Macdonald suggested that the same rule of 'read it, hide it and go back to it' applied. The important thing is to see what is being said, try and express it in the same form then see how well you have succeeded. The Alexandrine is not natural, otherwise more people would have used it. He felt that it is vital not to try and deny the origin of the source, i.e. *Phèdre* is a play by a Frenchman and he would tend to make the translation more foreign rather than less. It is something outside people's usual experience anyway, and this should be preserved. Similarly, it is mistaken to translate Berlin street language into Cockney as London and Berlin are different places. This tendency is a legacy from the 1960s 'we're all one' attitude. He preferred to maintain the Alexandrine in translation because that is its original form and if it sounds foreign, that is not necessarily a disadvantage.

TECHNICAL HITCHES

John Hayes, a freelance translator, suggested that Boris Uvarov had omitted writing ability from his list of requirements. He added that he had many doubts regarding the reliability of technical dictionaries as they were compiled by a handful of people and included their knowledge deficiencies. He asked Boris Uvarov how much the translator should edit source material – we all do it to some extent, but should we notify the client of editorial changes or should we do it off our own bat?

The answer was that it is wise to notify the client if something doesn't make sense in the original. As for the fourth requirement, Boris Uvarov felt that writing ability was implicit in the 'ability to present the result in the target language'.

ON A LIGHTER NOTE

Patricia Crampton asked Ewald Osers to expand on a remark he had once made about producing a translation of a given text that was identical to Michael Hamburger's. Ewald confirmed that this was true: the two translations of six lines of poetry were made independently and were identical – but this was only possible with a writer like Kunze who uses words with 'minimal penumbra' for which there are exact equivalents and strings them together. He avoids romantic vagueness. Such a degree of coincidence would be unlikely for any other author.

THE MISSING X FACTOR

Albin Tybulewicz, freelance translator and editor asked the panel if, in addition to the three prerequisites of a good translator, i.e. good knowledge of the source language, subject expertise and excellent command of the target language, there wasn't an indefinable fourth quality, a factor X which was also vital. Robert Macdonald felt that for a translator to achieve a lasting translation, he or she needs to be in sympathy or even empathy with the author – although this is less true for scientific translation. Professor Seleskovitch agreed that empathy was important but added that in the same way that every child can be taught to speak and write, good training can produce good translators and interpreters. Great writers have innate talent however and the same is true for translators. You cannot train literary translators who do not possess that essential quality.

Ewald Osers had the last word, saying that the way to diagnose the presence of the mysterious X factor was when a translator was tempted to translate something purely for the pleasure of producing a good translation even though it was unlikely to be published and he or she would not receive payment.

Session 5: The interpreting scene

Chaired by Valerie Anderson

The interpreter's job – a blow-by-blow account

Christiane-Jacqueline Driesen

Freelance interpreter

The paper is primarily concerned with the situation of court interpreting in Germany, bearing in mind that West Germany is made up of ten partially autonomous Länder. I am particularly interested in discussing methods and techniques with a view to improving the standard of our service, which is a vital element in the administration of justice. Finally I shall seek to describe briefly the various difficulties encountered in the past and consider the improvements we have been able to introduce in Hamburg, with reference to court interpreting qualifications and examination requirements.

I hope that my contributions will consolidate our dialogue in Europe on court interpreting and especially between the ITI and the BDÜ (Bundesverband der Dolmetscher und Ubersetzer), a dialogue which was started on an official level when Claire Kahtan, vice chairman of ITI, addressed a meeting in Hamburg attended by court interpreters, high court judges and police officers in which she described the situation of court interpreting in the United Kingdom.

PROCEDURE

The Offence

Place: a bar in Hamburg. Time: 1 a.m. Pierre Ducouteau is a long way from his native France, and living it up in Hamburg, but has drunk rather more than is good for him. Suddenly, a fight breaks out, and a man gets a knife between his ribs.

An incident which might happen anywhere – but the chain of legal events which it triggers off varies from one country to another. In Germany, procedure is basically like this:

The police or the public prosecutor may be informed of an offence by:

— Information laid by any member of the public, e.g. the proprietor of the bar (*Strafanzeige*).
— Information laid by the victim of the crime – in this case the man on the sharp end of the knife (*Strafantrag*).

— The offence comes to the notice of an official, e.g. a passing policeman sees the bloody deed being committed (*Amtliche Wahrnehmung*).

At the police station

A suspect – in our case Pierre Ducouteau – is apprehended, and immediately taken to the police station for questioning. In the course of routine formalities (taking of photographs, fingerprints, etc.), the officer in charge of the case realises that he will need the services of an interpreter. He scans the official list of sworn interpreters of the *Land* of Hamburg to find a French interpreter; it may be 3 a.m. but there is no time to lose. One phone call and fifteen minutes' drive later, the interpreter is ready for action.

The maximum period for which a suspect may be detained without being charged is twenty-four hours. If there seems to be good reason for detaining a person for longer than twenty-four hours, the suspect must be brought before a magistrate (*Amtsrichter*) before the expiry of this period, for a decision as to whether he may be held in custody.

In order for him to be held, the following conditions must be fulfilled:

— substantial grounds for believing that the suspect has committed the offence in question (*dringender Tatverdacht*)

and

— danger that the suspect might abscond (*Fluchtgefahr*); *or*
— danger that the suspect might obstruct the course of justice (*Verdunkelungsgefahr*); *or*
— danger of repetition of the alleged offence (*Wiederholungsgefahr*).

Questioning through an interpreter

Our interpreter is on the spot, still shaking off the last signs of sleep, and the officer in charge informs him or her briefly of what the case is about, and then calls for the suspect. In order to avoid any misunderstandings, the interpreter first explains to the suspect his/her role as a neutral interpreter.

The questioning proper starts with a caution (*Belehrung*), informing the suspect of his rights, which are roughly as follows:

1. he is informed what offence(s) he is suspected of committing;
2. he is informed that he may answer the officer's questions if he wishes but is not obliged to do so;
3. he is informed that he is entitled to insist on the presence of a lawyer at any time should he so desire.

If the officer in charge wishes to use a tape recording to record the interview, the suspect is asked whether he consents to this.

Even if he declines to answer the questions on points of fact, the suspect is obliged to answer questions as to his person. In our case, Pierre Ducouteau agrees to answer the officer's questions. The interpreter certifies that he has translated the caution for the suspect and signs the form; the suspect confirms that he has understood the translation and that he consents (or declines, as the case may be) to make a statement. The officer and Pierre Ducouteau face each other on either side of a desk, with the interpreter sitting at right-angles between them. Mostly, the officer types his (or her) own questions directly into a typewriter, followed by the German translations of the answers given by the suspect. Sometimes he will dictate into a dictaphone for subsequent transcription. The interpreter mostly translates in simultaneous 'whispering' technique, thus giving the speakers the impression of communicating directly with one another. This enables the officer to concentrate on Pierre Ducouteau's facial expression and tone of voice. There is no written translation question-by-question into the language of the suspect. When the interview is complete, the interpreter gives an at-sight translation of the entire written text as taken down by the officer. Pierre Ducouteau can then put forward any modifications or amendments that he wishes to make. If he agrees with the written record, he will then sign his statement; but he is not legally obliged to do so.

Remuneration of the interpreter

If the interpreter is still in a fit condition to do so, the officer will ask him or her to fill in a form in order to claim the remuneration. In many cases, the officer is kind enough to fill in this form for the interpreter. The form is for the payment of compensation (rather than fees, which would be too heavy a burden on the public purse) set out in the law on the compensation of experts and witnesses (*ZSEG*). The present hourly rate of remuneration, which is identical for work with the police and at court, varies between DM 40 and DM 70, depending on the difficulty of the particular assignment; in addition, interpreters who make their living as full-time interpreters are entitled to claim an additional payment of 40 to 50 per cent on top of this remuneration. The period for which remuneration is paid starts at the time of leaving home, and continues until the time of return. There are supplements for night work and for work on public holidays; travelling expenses are also paid.

Bringing the suspect before a magistrate (Haftrichter)

Assuming that Pierre Ducouteau fulfils the conditions for detention in custody, he will on the same day be brought before a magistrate (*Haftrichter*), who will have sole right of decision as to whether to allow further detention in custody. He will proceed in the same way as at the police station, calling an interpreter, who may be the same as the one who interpreted at the police station, and will inform the accused:

1. what offence(s) he is suspected of;
2. that he may answer the questions put to him but is not obliged to do so;
3. that he can at any time insist upon the presence of a lawyer of his choice.

Pierre Ducouteau is questioned, and the judge decides to remand him in custody, because the conditions – which are basically the same as those applicable for detention by the police – are fulfilled. Pierre Ducouteau was seen stumbling out of the bar with blood dripping from his hands; he has no dependents or relatives and no fixed abode in the Federal Republic of Germany, and is therefore deemed liable to abscond.

Preliminary proceedings *(Vorverfahren/Ermittlungsverfahren)*

During this period, the inquiry follows its course. This initial phase is placed under the authority of the public prosecutor, whose job it is to gather and get the police to gather as much evidence as possible to justify the indictment, which is the act initiating the main proceedings before a court.

Indictment* *(Anklageerhebung)*

And this is what happened a few months later in the case of Pierre Ducouteau. The public prosecutor filed the bill of indictment *(Anklageschrift)* against him with the competent court of jurisdiction.

The bill of indictment includes the following:

— details of the offence(s) alleged, giving date, place and time
— the legal relevance of these, and the legal provisions to be applied
— evidence to be presented (witnesses; expert's reports; exhibits)
— principal findings of the preliminary proceedings
— competent court of jurisdiction
— defending counsel.

Opening of the main proceedings

After receiving the bill of indictment (together with the dossier), the court forwards a copy of it – with a translation into French made by a sworn interpreter – to Pierre Ducouteau, asking him to state any objections or claims within a specified period. If necessary, Pierre Ducouteau is entitled to legal aid, and to ask for further information. In our case, the court finds that there is manifestly a *prima facie* case against Pierre Ducouteau, and decides to open the principal proceedings *(Hauptverfahren)*. By the date of the hearing, his victim has passed on to that great bar in the sky. The competent court is therefore the Criminal Senate of the County Court sitting in its composition with three professional judges and two lay judges *(Landgericht, große Kammer als Schwurgericht)*.

*The term 'indictment' is used here for *Anklageerhebung*, although the latter term is much broader; under German law there is no distinction between indictable offences, offences which are liable to summary trial, and offences triable either way.

Order of procedure − interpretation

1. The Presiding Judge calls the case, makes sure that all the protagonists are present − in particular an interpreter − and that the evidence is ready for hearing/inspection. He instructs the witnesses of their obligation to tell the truth, and explains to them the significance of the oath which they may be asked to take at the end of their testimony. The witnesses then leave the room (there is no special room set aside for the witnesses). In this phase, the interpreter whispers the translation to the accused. He/she gives a translation to the accused of everything that is said. This is to provide the accused with the same information as a German would have under the same circumstances. For certain major cases, simultaneous translation using full technical equipment with headphones may be used.

2. The Presiding Judge then establishes the identity of Pierre Ducouteau. The interpreter provides consecutive translation for the court, or sometimes uses whispering technique when translating for the accused.

3. The public prosecutor then reads the indictment (*Verlesung des Anklagesatzes*). The accused has a translated copy of this, but because of the principle of oral presentation of evidence, the interpreter gives an at-sight translation to the accused in whispering technique.

4. The Presiding Judge informs the accused of his right to remain silent as to the facts of which he is accused.

5. If the accused declares that he consents to answer the questions − which is the case for Pierre Ducouteau − the Presiding Judge asks him to give his version of the facts. No-one interrupts him during this initial phase. Everyone takes notes (judges, prosecuting counsel, etc.). The interpreter gives a consecutive translation, taking notes if necessary, since it is not admissible to deprive the accused of his right to make his statement without being interrupted.

   Once the accused has finished, the Presiding Judge starts asking him for explanations on certain points, then gives the floor to the other protagonists in turn, and they do the same. The tone of questioning may be insistent, but invariably remains polite. The interpreter uses consecutive or whispering technique, as appropriate.

6. The next stage is the hearing of evidence (*Beweisaufnahme*), and the testimony of witnesses and experts − in the case of Pierre Ducouteau, there are a number of physicians, a psychiatrist, and some arms specialists, with the presentation of exhibits, the knife, photos, etc. The interpreter uses simultaneous whispering technique, in order that Pierre Ducouteau will not miss any of what is going on, since the accused must be in a position to exercise his legal right of putting questions to any witness or expert.

7. The Presiding Judge terminates the taking of evidence, and calls upon the prosecutor and the defending counsel to make their final speeches. The interpreter translates these to the accused in whispering technique.

8.   The President gives the accused the right of saying the last word.
9.   The court (i.e. the judges and lay judges) retires to consider its verdict and sentence.
10. After a more or less lengthy delay, the court returns and the verdict is pronounced. Everyone in court is upstanding. The translation is given in simultaneous whispering technique, in order not to keep the accused waiting for too long. Everyone then sits down again to listen to the Presiding Judge's explanation of reasons for the verdict and – if applicable – the sentence.

No doubt you have noticed that it is up to the interpreter to decide what interpreting techniques to use; and that these techniques are the basic techniques of conference interpreting – consecutive and simultaneous. The object of the exercise is to put the non-German-speaker as far as possible into the same position as a German appearing before the court.

However, the conditions of communication in court are very different from the conditions that apply at international conferences; the main difference being the tremendous socio-cultural gap that exists between foreigners and nationals appearing before the court. Just compare the example of a conference interpreter at, for example, an international conference on plastics. He or she is working for specialists who share more or less the same background (basically similar education and training, specialist knowledge and professional experience); and it is the exception for these specialists to depart from the world of hard facts and make an appeal to the emotions. The only advantage which the interpreter has over these specialists is a knowledge of languages. In court, the interpreter cannot provide valid communication between the parties unless he or she manages – on however limited a scale – to bridge the socio-cultural gap that separates those involved. Hence it is not sufficient for the interpreter to restrict himself or herself to purely linguistic interpretation; the provisions of Articles 3.1 and 3.3 of the Basic Law of the Federal Republic of Germany, state that 'All persons shall be equal before the law' and 'No-one may be prejudiced or favoured because of his sex, his parentage, his race, his language, his homeland and origin, his faith, or his religious or political opinions'.

In order to comply with the law, the interpreter must constantly check and ensure that he or she has been properly understood both by the accused and by the court. If this is not the case, it is up to him or her to do the following:

— to get the persons concerned to raise an appropriate question; or
— to get the Presiding Judge to give the relevant explanation; or
— to obtain authorisation to give the relevant explanation if this appears indispensable in order to avoid a misunderstanding. This could be an explanation to the court (in the capacity of an expert) or it could be to the accused.

The court permits and appreciates discreet interventions of this kind on the part of a competent and courteous interpreter.

I hope this brief introduction will have given you an idea of the qualifications needed to become a sworn interpreter in the Federal Republic of Germany:

— perfect command of the language-pair concerned
— mastery of the standard techniques of interpretation
— legal and cultural knowledge of the two linguistic regions involved
— a high standard of professional ethics.

CONDITIONS FOR RECRUITMENT OF SWORN INTERPRETERS IN WEST GERMANY; WEAKNESSES OF THE SYSTEM

Unfortunately, at the present time there are not many interpreters in West Germany who fulfil the conditions listed above. There are two major reasons for this.

The first is that each *Land* is entitled to lay down its own rules and regulations for the selection of interpreters and translators to work for the authorities. This means that conditions are extremely disparate from one part of the country to another. Depending on the particular *Land*, selection is made by:

— application to the President of the County Court; or
— submission of professional certificates, etc.; or
— sitting an examination — this is the procedure applied in Munich and Hamburg . . . and it is the best procedure!

The translator and/or interpreter then takes an official oath — this is a once-and-for-all oath which remains valid for an indefinite period. The translator/interpreter receives an official document certifying the fact, and in certain *Länder* — in particular in Hamburg — he or she also receives an official seal, which is used to certify officially that the translations he or she has made are true and complete translations of the respective original.

The second reason is that the courts and the police are in no way obliged to avail themselves of the services of sworn interpreters. The judge is always entitled to swear in any person that he or she believes competent, on an ad hoc basis. What he or she does in practice is to ask the clerk of the court to obtain the services of — say — an interpreter for Spanish, at such and such a time on such and such a date. Perhaps the clerk of the court knows that a friend's daughter has been in Barcelona for six months as au pair, on the strength of which that friend has declared his daughter to be an interpreter; the clerk of the court will thereupon call the girl as interpreter. If the latter's Spanish sounds sufficiently foreign that no-one in the court understands a word she is saying – apart from the accused, who will possibly not dare to protest – the girl will be all set to start on her career as a pseudo-interpreter.

A PROMISING SOLUTION IN HAMBURG

The kind of situation that I have just described is what led the BDÜ, and in particular its Hamburg Section, to launch a real campaign of action for reform. This campaign has recently been crowned with success in the *Land* of Hamburg, since we have succeeded in getting a new law passed and a new ordinance enacted governing the way that sworn interpreters and translators are selected. These set out the official procedure for examining the knowledge of persons aspiring to these functions:

— linguistic knowledge – mainly tested by written translation
— legal knowledge
— techniques of interpretation (simultaneous, consecutive and translation at sight)
— professional ethics (interview)

The examiners are a panel of two interpreters and translators, a representative of the university specialising in the language in question, and two representatives of the users (a civil servant and/or a judge, or a public prosecutor, or a police official).

CONCLUSION

I have tried to give a practical account of the role and responsibilities of the interpreter in the administration of criminal justice in West Germany. I have covered:

— conditions of recruitment
— necessary qualifications for efficient performance of the work required
— conditions for exercise of these functions with the police and at court
— remuneration.

You will no doubt have observed that the situation is about as unsatisfactory as it is everywhere in the world, but that there are professionals committed to struggle for improvement of conditions. I have likewise suggested in what direction the professional group constituted within the BDÜ believes it should continue its work on a national level.

In presenting this paper, I have been aiming to continue the dialogue – still a rather tentative one – that certain professionals are trying to initiate, in Europe to start with. In Hamburg we hosted a European Forum on Court Interpreting in 1982; then we invited the Dutch association NGV for an exchange of views; and, earlier this year, we had the very great pleasure of welcoming Claire Kahtan, a member of the ITI Council, to talk to us about the problems of court and police interpreting in Britain. This event turned out to be a remarkable success — as at the previous meetings, we invited not only colleagues in the profession, but also judges, lawyers and police officials. Each time, this led to a deepening of understanding of the problems on the part of the users, who were given a new insight into the interpreter's profession and the difficulties it involves. If, with this paper, I have made any contribution to sowing some seeds of insight, I will be more than satisfied with that result.

APPENDIX 1

ORGANISATION OF THE JUDICIARY IN GERMANY

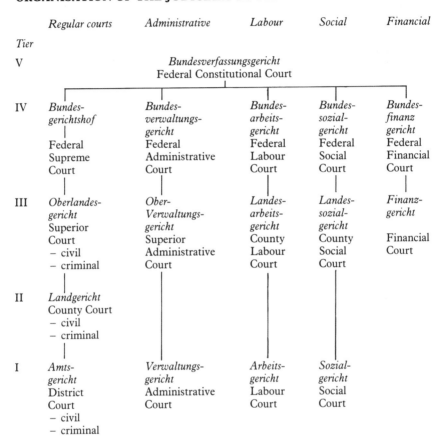

Tier	*Regular courts*	*Administrative*	*Labour*	*Social*	*Financial*
V		*Bundesverfassungsgericht* Federal Constitutional Court			
IV	*Bundes-gerichtshof* Federal Supreme Court	*Bundes-verwaltungs-gericht* Federal Administrative Court	*Bundes-arbeits-gericht* Federal Labour Court	*Bundes-sozial-gericht* Federal Social Court	*Bundes-finanz gericht* Federal Financial Court
III	*Oberlandes-gericht* Superior Court – civil – criminal	*Ober-Verwaltungs-gericht* Superior Administrative Court	*Landes-arbeits-gericht* County Labour Court	*Landes-sozial-gericht* County Social Court	*Finanz-gericht* Financial Court
II	*Landgericht* County Court – civil – criminal				
I	*Amts-gericht* District Court – civil – criminal	*Verwaltungs-gericht* Administrative Court	*Arbeits-gericht* Labour Court	*Sozial-gericht* Social Court	

APPENDIX 2

STRUCTURE OF THE CRIMINAL COURTS IN GERMANY

The courts of the Federal Republic of Germany are composed of:

1. Professional judges *(Berufsrichter)*
Conditions for appointment as a professional judge:
— must be a German national
— considered likely to uphold respect for the constitution
— qualified for the office of judge, i.e. must have passed two examinations — the first covering the contents of university law studies over a period of three and a half years, the second after a further two years of on-the-job training (comparable with 'taking articles').

2. Lay judges *(Schöffen)*
Conditions for appointment as a lay judge (honorary office):
— must be a German national
— nomination on a list drawn up by the municipality every four years
— election by a lay bench appointment committee *(Schöffenauswahlausschuß)* made up of various judges, civil servants and 10 persons of good public repute (*'Vertrauenspersonen'*).
The committee ensures that all groups of the population are represented (women, vocational groups, etc.).

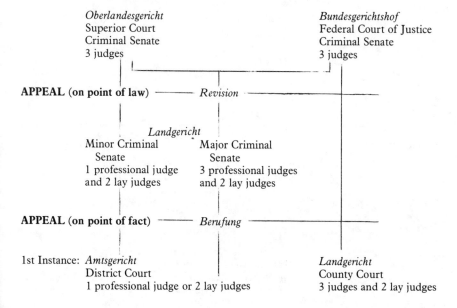

Oberlandesgericht
Superior Court
Criminal Senate
3 judges

Bundesgerichtshof
Federal Court of Justice
Criminal Senate
3 judges

APPEAL (on point of law) ——— *Revision*

Landgericht
Minor Criminal   Major Criminal
Senate   Senate
1 professional judge   3 professional judges
and 2 lay judges   and 2 lay judges

APPEAL (on point of fact) ——— *Berufung*

1st Instance: *Amtsgericht*   *Landgericht*
District Court   County Court
1 professional judge or 2 lay judges   3 judges and 2 lay judges

APPENDIX 3a

1. TYPICAL COURTROOM LAYOUT

Große Strafkammer – Major Criminal Senate of a higher court

1st alternative:

	Schöffe	*Richter*	*Vorsitzender*	*Richter*	*Schöffe*
	Lay Judge	Judge	Presiding Judge	Judge	Lay Judge

Gerichts-schreiber
Clerk

Angeklagter – Dolmetscher
Accused – Interpreter

Verteidiger   *Staatsanwalt*
Defending   Prosecutor
counsel

P U B L I C

2nd alternative:

	Schöffe	*Richter*	*Vorsitzender*	*Richter*	*Schöffe*
	Lay Judge	Judge	Presiding Judge	Judge	Lay Judge

Gerichts-schreiber
Clerk

Zeuge oder Sachverständiger
Witness or Expert
Angeklagter – Dolmetscher
Verteidiger   Accused – Interpreter   *Staatsanwalt*
Defending   Prosecutor
counsel

P U B L I C

3rd alternative:

	Schöffe	*Richter*	*Vorsitzender*	*Richter*	*Schöffe*
	Lay Judge	Judge	Presiding Judge	Judge	Lay Judge

Gerichts-schreiber
Clerk

Zeuge – Dolmetscher
Witness – Interpreter
Verteidiger   *Angeklagter – Dolmetscher*   *Staatsanwalt*
Defending   Accused – Interpreter   Prosecutor
counsel

P U B L I C

APPENDIX 3b

PROCEDURE IN COURT

1. The **Presiding Judge** conducts the proceedings. His or her job is not to act as a neutral 'umpire' but actively to inquire into the events and their interpretation.

2. There is **no 'cross examination'**. The accused and witnesses are first invited to put their view of the facts. They do this without being interrupted. Only after this does the Presiding Judge ask for further explanations and put more detailed questions. He or she then invites each of the judges to speak (including the lay judges), then the prosecutor, then the defending counsel(s), and — where a witness has been testifying — finally the accused.

   Prosecutor: same training as judges.

   Defending counsel: One and the same lawyer (*RA = Rechtsanwalt*) responsible for preparing and presenting case, roughly equivalent to barrister/solicitor in one.

3. There is a **lack of ceremony**. Clothing is very restrained — all members of the legal profession are dressed in black gowns; the judges and the prosecutor wear black velvet collars and a white tie (men) or scarf (women).

   The protagonists remain seated most of the time.

   The witnesses, experts and the accused testify from a seated position, standing only to take the oath; the public stand only when the judges enter the court room, when an oath is being taken, and when the verdict/sentence is pronounced.

   The prosecutor stands to read the bill of indictment and to make his or her speeches. The defending counsels stand to make their speeches.

4. **Oaths**. Sworn interpreters, experts and lay judges have taken an oath once and for all, and do not retake their oath for each session; they simply 'invoke the oath taken' (*berufen sich auf das geleistete Eid*).

   The witnesses are cautioned *before* their testimony of the sanctions for false testimony and perjury, and also of *their right to remain silent* rather than give evidence which might incriminate themselves. They take their oath only after giving testimony, and only if the other protagonists specifically request that they should do so. This procedure is indicative of the exceptional character of the oath.

Interpreting – the future

Liese Katschinka

Chairman, FIT Committee for Interpreters, Vienna, Austria

Since the Second World War, professional interpreting has become an established feature of multilingual relations. In keeping with user needs, the profession has developed several profiles (simultaneous interpreting, consecutive interpreting; conference interpreting, business interpreting, court interpreting, media interpreting, community interpreting, etc.), requiring specific skills and approaches. Technical progress, social change and newly emerging needs for interpretation services will result in a further diversification of the profession. The paper discusses several phenomena that are of relevance to the future of interpreting.

INTRODUCTION

'Interpreting is the second-oldest profession in the world'. I am sure that you have heard this saying many times before and that, every time you heard it, you were just as pleased about its implications as I am whenever I hear or read it. Sometimes you hear 'Translating is the second-oldest profession in the world' – but this slight variation is mainly due to the fact that, to this very day, the public at large has not become aware that interpreting involves speaking, while translating involves writing.

My topic is interpreting, the future of interpreting to be precise, and my seemingly frivolous introduction does not mean that I will deal with the subject in a light-hearted or entertaining manner. On the contrary, the introduction is meant to put my subject into perspective: before you discuss the future, you should look to the past, and you should describe the present situation.

BACKGROUND

Without going back to ancient Egypt, where we find first proof of the interpreting profession [1], and without discussing the role of interpreters in European history [2], I think it is fair to say that interpreting is indeed a time-honoured profession: at all times, whenever people of different languages wanted to communicate, they found someone familiar with foreign languages, who helped them to speak to each other. Depending on the civilisation, interpreters had a higher or lower status in society. Since the needs for interpretation were fairly limited, interpreting was not a full-scale profession. The people who had acquired foreign language skills became self-made interpreters, i.e. they devised their own techniques for interpreting, which was essentially consecutive interpreting (with or without note-taking).

Interpreting remained more or less unchanged until modern means of transport made travelling a common feature of most people's lives, and until modern means of technology made multi-lingual exchanges an easily accessible form of communication. As a result, politicians, civil servants, scientists, businessmen, artists, etc., do get together more often than ever before, and in any city, seaside resort or Alpine village they like, in order to discuss the problems which they have in common. By putting on their earphones and tuning in to the language channel of their choice, they need not worry about losing time understanding each other. With the explosion of the congress industry after the Second World War, interpreters are no longer regarded as rare and exotic birds; rather, they have become familiar faces – useful links in the communication chain.

PRESENT SITUATION

What has this meant for the profession, how does this evolution affect the status of interpreters? Well, gone are the days of the Russian aristocrats who grew up speaking French to their parents and Russian to their servants, while learning English from their nanny and German from their tutor. When they became interpreters, after the Russian Revolution had forced them to abandon their family estates, the League of Nations and other institutions were happy to benefit from their language skills, and politicians throughout the world appreciated their suave manners at official functions. Their personalities afforded them a position of prestige in society. Maybe that is the origin of a common belief that interpreting is a glamour profession.

Also gone, or almost gone, are the days of a first generation of interpreters who acquired their language skills through the vicissitudes of life, caused by the upheavals in Europe before and during the Second World War. When they began their interpreting careers, they were smart enough to realise that the profession needed certain standards, to be respected and applied universally, if top-quality interpretation was to be separated from dilettante dabbling in foreign languages. It is that generation of interpreters which made it possible for interpreting fees to be negotiated with international organisations, for manning tables to be standardised and for university departments to be set up to train interpreters. On account of their commitment to the profession as such, interpreting became a full-fledged profession, which could be exercised until normal retirement age (or even beyond). They set the yardstick for the next generation of interpreters: having obtained proper training in modern inter-preting skills and operating under decent working conditions, interpreters could provide language-communication services of increasingly better quality.

The 1950s and 1960s were a seller's market. Those interpreters were wise enough to sell their services shrewdly and prudently. We owe them our gratitude for being able to walk into well-ventilated, properly insulated booths of adequate dimensions, to sit down on comfortable chairs and at well-lit desks, to adjust our lightweight earphones, and to listen to speakers that we can see, while our interpretation is transmitted to an audience that has realised, to some extent, that interpreters are not parrots.

Of course, the above picture is drawn in bright colours. I should not forget the dark spots on the canvas: we still find booths that are cubbyholes, where you either freeze or suffocate, desks where you bruise your knees or tear your stockings, or chairs that make your back ache before the first coffee-break. And when you take off your earphones to rummage among the conference documents on the dusty floor, you realise that your headache has become worse.

But, by and large, it was much easier for the next generation of interpreters to embark upon a career in interpreting. With some good sense, they could even steer clear of the frustrations which this new profession can cause, like never seeing the town to which you have come for an assignment, always hurrying to catch the earliest train or plane, or broken marriages, alienated friends, and tickets to a special theatre performance which must go unused because you are scheduled to interpret at a late-night session.

Since learning languages, and using languages as a profession, attracted an increasing number of women, male interpreters have become a minority. Sociologists will tell you that a profession begins to lose some of its social prestige, once it is exercised primarily by women. I wonder how much status the interpreting profession lost towards the late 1970s and early 1980s because of the large number of female interpreters. I also wonder to what extent the working standards of the profession are gradually declining because a constantly growing number of schools is grinding out ever larger quantities of graduates in interpretation, who are eager to make a living but have little consideration for the ethics of the profession. Perhaps interpreters should be more aware of these dangers to the profession, maybe the next time when a potential client asks them 'to help out a little' with the dinner-table conversation after a meeting – no extra fee involved, of course. Without wanting to sound like a feminist, I would wish young interpreters to develop a healthy sense of self-esteem. If you want to be taken for a professional, you must behave like a professional – and your work should come up to professional standards.

PRESENT TRENDS

After this brief review of the historical background of the interpreting profession – in very general terms, of course – I come to the present-day situation, where I can see two major tendencies:

1. a changing market.
2. a need for new forms of interpreting.

A changing market

In many ways, today's market is a buyer's market. With the economic crisis, international organisations, government departments and other clients have to make do with tighter budgets for congresses, seminars, meetings, press conferences, product presentations, etc. Whenever possible, they will reduce the number of working languages to a minimum, they will commit themselves and sign contracts as late as possible, they will shop around for less expensive options, or they will recruit locals instead of hiring the team that they used to take along to previous conferences. They have also learnt that excursions (without interpreters) should better be scheduled before or after a conference, that starting a meeting in the afternoon (or closing it at lunch-time) might save them *per noctems*, and that the sole delegate from Italy can listen to a whispered interpretation and does not need simultaneous interpretation. To some extent, this attitude may also be a reaction to the often excessive demands advanced by thoughtless interpreters who do not even bother to find out what the client needs. The new generation of interpretation users in the private market wants tailor-made solutions for its interpretation needs. They ask recruiting interpreters for their advice early, and they are willing to accept programme changes recommended by interpreters.

The interpreting profession has also gone through a process of secularisation. What do I mean by that? − Of course, Reagan and Gorbachev will continue to negotiate with the help of interpreters, but Commissioner Declerq spoke English when addressing a group of top-echelon bankers in Austria recently, and there was no interpretation at all. There are fewer glitzy assignments; interpreting is fast becoming a bread-and-butter profession. In the past, a conference interpreter (preferably an attractive female) was hired on many occasions for the small talk among business executives in two or more foreign languages, or 'to be around, just in case language difficulties should arise'. They were some kind of trimming for the event. This market segment is shrinking, while new markets are emerging.

A need for new forms of interpreting

The changing needs of the market have triggered a diversification of the interpreting profession. The more selective user community encouraged this evolution, and imaginative interpreters began to test various alternatives to the traditional interpreting skills. The volume of required interpretation services is not declining but changing, and interpreters should be aware of the challenges and be prepared to adjust to them.

Let me give you a few examples:

1. *Interpreting for the media.* When SFT and ITI organised their joint seminar on translating and interpreting for the media in February 1988 [3], the speakers demonstrated convincingly that television and broadcasting companies have a growing demand for interpreters. Interpreters should, however, not only be capable of interpreting (simultaneously or consecutively) but they should also be able to 'moderate' a live transmission in a foreign language, to 'edit' an interview for the evening news, or to write and read the commentary on the film which is being dubbed. Consequently, they must know how to work with television or video equipment, and they must be able to 'write' and 'speak' their own texts. By using their ingenuity, and testing different approaches, interpreters will eventually be in a position to define these new skills. The university departments which have started to train this new species of interpreters will be able to benefit from their first-hand experience.

2. *Interpreting for the business community.* The number of business transactions between companies in different countries of the world has increased dramatically during recent decades. But if the business partners negotiate their transactions in a foreign language, misunderstandings and disputes can be the result which need to be examined by arbitration tribunals. Simultaneous interpretation is fast becoming a popular recourse when conducting arbitral proceedings, since it will improve their expediency. When accepting assignments of this kind, interpreters should be aware that lawyers have their own vernacular, that preparing the case means understanding the issue and not reading hundreds of pages, and that every word counts if the award involves millions of dollars. I feel that the demands on an interpreter's concentration are so great under these circumstances that at least one more interpreter should be added to the team. After all, when it is not your turn to interpret, you must continue to follow the case. As in business negotiations, interpreters will occasionally also be involved in drafting or editing the minutes – a task which requires special attention, since the written text must reflect the shades of meaning that were so obvious when a witness gave his testimony. This increasingly emerging form of interpretation requires more personal involvement on the part of the interpreter, and is more rewarding in many ways, since the interpreter is closely associated with the progress of the case.

3. *Interpreting for the courts and the police.* Law courts are another group of customers that use simultaneous interpretation increasingly when conducting hearings and interrogating defendants. Conversely, interpreters are discovering that simultaneous interpretation may be a good alternative to sitting next to a terrorist or murderer for several days. In this connection, being a woman may be an asset in convincing the court to use simultaneous equip-

ment. Whether conducted with the help of consecutive or simultaneous interpretation, court proceedings are becoming more frequent and more complex. Interpreter training schools should provide specific programmes, so that interpreting for the courts will become an attractive career option for future interpreters. At the same time, legislators should redefine the qualifications for court interpreters and upgrade their remuneration schemes. Let's try to break out of the present vicious circle which implies that only second-class interpreters will work for the courts or the police, because the pay is only second or third class. Court and police interpreters should cease to be regarded as the poor cousins of conference interpreters. In some cases, their assignments involve more responsibility than certain simultaneous interpretation jobs, for example the 27th General Assembly of the European Federation of Bottlecap Producers at Marbella. Why be so penny-wise and pound-foolish? I hope that M.J. Velasco-Ulazia's initiative for an EC directive on court interpreting and translating will eventually improve the situation [4].

Interpreting for ethnic minorities

Social security officers, physicians and nurses, school principals or highway patrolmen, and their respective counterparts are another emerging user group. How can the registrar's assistant tell the unskilled worker from Turkey to produce the birth certificates of his dozen children, how can the truck driver from Portugal tell the police that poisonous chemicals are leaking from his upturned truck, and how should the physician find out about his patient's complaints, if that patient speaks nothing but Urdu? Of course, there is usually a relative or friend around who can help to overcome the language barriers. On many occasions, though, the results of such good neighbourly assistance are not very satisfactory. Local authorities, or hospitals, prefer increasingly to have a qualified team of community interpreters at their disposal. Particularly in the more exotic languages, efficient and reliable interpreters are still a scarcity. Roger Fletcher, himself an interpreter for Chinese, reported about Ann Corsellis' work in Cambridgeshire in training community interpreters with the generous support of the Nuffield Foundation, at the XIth World Congress of FIT at Maastricht in August 1987 [5]. A thorough knowledge of the socio-cultural background of the foreign-language user and a thorough knowledge of the context of the assignment are needed, in addition to excellent foreign-language skills (especially regional accents and dialects), to produce a top-quality community interpreter. Here again, working conditions and payment schemes should be upgraded to reflect the responsibilities involved in these foreign-language communication services.

Interpreting for the hearing-handicapped

Last, not least, we should mention visual-language interpreting. The hearing-handicapped are no longer resigned to their quiet corner of the house but want to be 'listened to' and have a more active part in community affairs. *Children of a Lesser God* and the Oscar award to the leading actress in that film have helped to generate more understanding for the problems of the deaf and dumb. They too, need interpreters to communicate with the world around them. If sign-language interpreting were a recognised profession, and if there were more programmes like J.G. Kyle's at the University of Bristol [6], more young people would turn to visual-language interpretation. The result would be more efficient and more frequent interpreting services for these less-privileged members of society.

SUMMING UP

The market for interpretation services is changing, and new forms of interpreting are emerging. After the Second World War, AIIC (*Association Internationale des Interprètes de Conférence*) and – to a lesser degree – FIT played a leading part in advancing the profession. The elected officers of these two international organisations were committed to 'a good cause'. They focused their efforts on a specific goal, i.e. to establish standards for the profession. Eventually, their personal input of energy, dedication and time produced a tangible output for the individual interpreter (and translator): decent working conditions, decent remuneration rates and a better social status. Having achieved that objective, they seem to have little enthusiasm left for any further activities.

Today, several national associations of professional interpreters and translators seem to have assumed the responsibility for promoting the new interpreting skills. The initiative is no longer with the conference interpreters but with those exercising the newly emerging interpreting skills. They must convince the TV executive, for example, that he or she should hire an interpreter to edit a video tape, or the police officer that he or she should assign a professional interpreter to an interrogation. The hour of interpreting service will cost more but the job will probably be finished in less time.

It's these little steps that count right now, and they can be taken only on a national level – of course, with the support of the international organisations. There is no need for international declarations that remain empty words on a piece of paper.

Community interpreters, media interpreters, court interpreters, etc., should also have the benefit of the experience gained by the conference interpreters when improving their working standards. Cooperation among the different types of interpreters can only help to avoid any rivalries or misunderstandings.

I would also wish for the future that there were more interpreters' schools willing to experiment with new curricula, and interpreters willing to share their experience in the newly emerging interpreting skills.

CONCLUSION

If you were expecting me to give statistics on how many days of work the UN or the EC will provide by 1990, or whether you can improve your career opportunities by learning Hungarian or Swahili, you may be disappointed. When accepting the invitation to address your Congress, I told the organisers that I was not involved in any research project on the present subject but that I was a freelance interpreter, and that I would share with you my experience of twenty years in the profession, and of three years as Chairman of the FIT Committee for Interpreters.

REFERENCES

[1] KURZ, I. Das Dolmetscher-Relief aus dem Grab des Haremhab in Memphis. Ein Beitrag zur Geschichte des Dolmetschens im alten Ägypten. *Babel*, No. 2/1986, pp. 215-221.
[2] THIEME, K. Die Bedeutung des Dolmetschens für die Weltgeschichte Europeas. *Beiträge zur Geschichte des Dolmetschens, Schriften des Auslands- und Dolmetscher-instituts der Johannes-Gutenberg-Universität Mainz in Germersheim.* Munich: Isar Verlag, 1956.
[3] La traduction face aux nouveaux medias, organised by SFT and ITI, Paris, February 20-21, 1988.
[4] Compte rendu des réunions du Conseil de la FIT, Paris, May 28–June 1, 1987.
[5] CORSELLIS, A., Community Interpreter Project, XIth FIT Congress, Maastricht, August 24-27, 1987.
[6] University of Bristol, Certificate in Sign Language Interpreting, November 1987.

Session 6: Translators' forum

Chaired by Charles Polley

Chairman's introduction

Charles Polley

Freelance translator

> Almost every product or service requires some translator involvement. This forum critically examines the financial viability of translation activities, seeking conclusions of benefit both to freelance and staff translators. The freelance has only so many hours in the day. How can they be put to effective use? Staff translators provide services to their employers. Can work be better arranged to meet the aspirations of translator and employer alike? Are translators undervalued, or about to be recognised as the hidden lubricant in the economic machine? Panel members will share their suggestions. The audience is invited to expand the picture.

Welcome to this, the first of the two forum sessions. Our topic is 'productivity equals profits', and like all good subjects for discussion, there is an implicit question mark after the title.

Almost every product or service you may care to mention requires some involvement with translators at a given stage in its development. This forum enables you, the members of the audience, to examine the financial viability of translation activities, and to ask whether translators are undervalued, or about to be recognised as the hidden lubricant in the economic machine, especially in the context of 1992 and beyond.

Let me start by saying this: We may all know some wealthy translators, but it's almost certain they didn't get to be wealthy just by translating! There has to be some other dimension – some extra ingredient we would all like to know about (not least of all myself) – for improving productivity and therefore, presumably, profits.

In Session 1 we heard a lot about target-oriented translation. Similarly, in the general area of profitability we do well to remember that those who use our services do so themselves to gain some extra competitive edge which will help them to improve their own profitability.

If we are to equate productivity with profits, it is as well to define what we mean. I will give some official definitions, and leave you to judge how far they apply to your own individual case. The *International dictionary of management* [1] defines productivity as follows: 'The relationship between input and output of an industrial unit etc, input being measured in men, machines, materials and money, and output in products and services. Reliable methods of productivity measurement are elusive but various ad hoc yardsticks have been produced'. Of productivity ratios it says: 'Relating physical input measures to output gives productivity ratios. They may include output per man and output per unit of material used. Physical input measures for labour may be people, attendance hours or paid hours.' On the other hand, William Davis, in his book *Money talks* [2], defined productivity as: 'What you can get out of a man – and his machine – within a given period. Anything wider usually comes under the heading of "efficiency".' Whilst acknowledging the quaintly sexist tones of these definitions, it does seem to me that today's discussions are almost certain to embrace the wider heading of efficiency, because inevitably we shall be looking at a number of matters including but not confined to investment in technology.

When you boil it all down, profit is essential. It is certain we shall not be able to count on more *time* for coping with requirements, since the 25-hour day plus the 8-day week are actually a myth, despite what our experience and even our commonsense might tell us! Perhaps we have to develop the art of being able to do a number of things at once – what you might call walking and chewing gum at the same time! Today, in fact, is no exception. We have very little time available for discussing this vast topic. In the brief span of this meeting, can we hope to assemble at least something of value which we can take away from here and use for the future? Well, we shall certainly try. Between them, our panel members have a fund – indeed a wealth – of ideas and experience, and soon they will be sharing some initial thoughts with us, briefly, as a stimulus for our discussions. But with the best will in the world, please do not assume they will come up with miracle solutions. They cannot do our thinking for us.

But now it is a pleasure to introduce the members of your panel. They are: Florence Herbulot and Lanna Castellano. Lanna Castellano is a freelance translator and a member of ITI Council. She campaigns vigorously for the profession, working for mutual support among members of the ITI and the promotion of ITI services, for example by launching language and subject networks. As an exponent of advice and counselling for new entrants to the profession, Lanna was a prime mover in the 'guardian angel' scheme. In line with her belief in the importance of professional development, she encourages workshops and persuades educational establishments to provide specific training for all stages of career development. Lanna also fosters cooperation with good translation agencies and other translation users, and encourages cross-linking with our colleagues in other national associations. (She also finds time to translate!)

Florence Herbulot is a fulltime technical and literary freelance translator. She holds a Translator's Diploma in English and Italian, and a doctorate in the science of interpreting and translating from the *Ecole Supérieure d'Interprètes et de Traducteurs* at the University of Paris III, where she is currently in charge of the Translation Section. The author of some ninety published translations and several thousand pages of translated technical literature, Florence was President of the *Société Française des Traducteurs* for six years and is a founding member of the ITI.

One possible area for us to examine is the kind of investment we need to make in ourselves and in developing our career paths. Our first speaker for the session, Lanna Castellano, has some thoughts on these and related topics.

Another possible route to greater productivity might be to find ways of increasing speed and accuracy in the way we work. Our second panel member, Florence Herbulot has some ideas on the subject.

REFERENCES

[1] JOHANNSEN, H. and PAGE, G. *International dictionary of management*. London: Kogan Page, 1986.
[2] DAVIS, W. *Money talks – a dictionary of money*. Revised edition. London: André Deutsch, 1974.

Get rich – but slow

Lanna Castellano

Freelance translator

As an optimist – a qualified optimist – my theme here is

GET RICH . . . BUT SLOW

There are two stages in a translator's career:

> *First*: a long apprenticeship – investing in yourself
> *Second*: cashing in on the investment

A LONG APPRENTICESHIP

If your value as a translator were really reflected in the rate you charge, you should be earning £1 per thousand words per year of your age.

Our profession is based on knowledge and experience. It has the longest apprenticeship of any profession. Not until thirty do you start to be useful as a translator, not until fifty do you start to be in your prime.

The first stage of the career pyramid – the apprenticeship stage – is the time we devote to *investing in ourselves* by acquiring knowledge and experience of life. Let me propose a life path: grandparents of different nationalities, a good school education in which you learn to read, write, spell, construe and love your own language. Then roam the world, make friends, see life. Go back to education, but to take a technical or commercial degree, not a language degree. Spend the rest of your twenties and your early thirties in the countries whose languages you speak, working in industry or commerce but not directly in languages. Never marry into your own nationality. Have your children. Then back to a postgraduate translation course. A staff job as a translator, and then go freelance. By which time you are forty and ready to begin.

There is no longer a place for the person who knows languages and how to translate them, but knows nothing else. The generalist has all but disappeared . . . and a good thing too. Do you want to spend your life juggling words but not meaning, acquiring itsy-bitsy knowledge of a thousand subjects? Today we are not translators but medical translators, legal translators, engineering translators. As we have found in our specialist workshops and seminars, our language and translation ability is our core skill, but it has to be combined with other skills to be of value.

At SFT's seminar on translation and the media, during Expolangues in Paris early in 1988, the lesson was that a media translator needs translation *plus* . . . plus copywriting ability and experience of the advertising world; . . . plus the experience and expertise acquired by working in and understanding television. In his talk on how to become a legal translator in London in January 1988, Ian Frame advised a correspondence course in law and a couple of years working in a notary's or solicitor's office. As we see from the demand – the unsatisfied demand – for software translators, an infotech translator needs language *plus* computer expertise.

The great investment, then, is training – and not just initial training. Sir John Harvey-Jones, former Chairman of ICI, says that not a year of his life has passed without going on courses and seminars to learn from experts in other fields. The importance of initial training may be over-stressed – a reaction to the time when there was *no* training to be a translator. Even more important is continuing training, lifelong training. Training in subject knowledge, if possible in a country using your adopted language. An admirable example is set by those Norwegian and Dutch colleagues of ours who come to England for at least a week each year for the Polytechnic of Central London's course on English law. And training includes seminars, workshops, conferences such as this, contact with others . . . and it's tax-deductible or payable by the employer. For rigorous study of a subject at your own pace and to fit in with your own working life, there are distance learning methods . . . for example the new Open College in Britain, which offers tuition in vocational subjects.

To go back to the ideal career pattern, only when you're young should you be a generalist, but for the sake of learning and for easing gently into the specialist field you prefer. Say yes to everything. Work for the agencies, but if possible for those agencies which really do revise. Insist on retyping the work they revise, whatever the time it takes you. Learning is a privilege, to be paid for. But gradually specialise. As you have more to offer, learn to say no. Don't prostitute yourself, after you're forty.

CASHING IN ON THE INVESTMENT

Are you as rich as you deserve to be? If not, why not? Let me propose a plan of action for *doing better, earning more*:

Analyse yourself

Why aren't you rich? Do you have all the work you can handle? Do you work slowly, say 2,000 words – eight pages – a day or less? Do you work all hours of the day and night, produce a large volume, but still earn a paltry £1,000 a month? Do you actually know what you produce, or your target for what you should earn?

If you were a business and your performance was lower than it could be, the first thing your bank manager would advise you would be: gather the facts.

Analyse your market

Ask the work providers: is it easy to find a translator who can be relied on to produce a good, accurate, professional piece of work, professionally presented, on a specialist subject, in a reasonably short time? No, it is not. And yet there are so many translators looking for work. Why does the supply not match the demand? Not hard to answer: because most translators are not good enough, not specialised enough, not professional enough, not well enough qualified, not well enough equipped or not motivated enough. Are you good, specialised, professional, equipped and motivated? If so, you can choose your clients. Go where the money is, to agencies if they will pay you a decent rate and take over the administrative worries. If English is your mother tongue, sell yourself to a country where English is prized. Translate for Germany, for Switzerland. Attract buyers by being part of a group, a language- or subject-network.

Set your goals

What do you want? More work? More work in your specialist field? A better quality of life – less work at a decent rate for better clients? Your self-analysis should show you how you fall short.

Run yourself like a business, even if you are a one-person business. Do what only *you* can do – translate – and delegate to others what others do better, or at least more economically, than you: book-keeping, delivering translations, filing, typing perhaps (a doubtful perhaps).

Is your output low – say, 2,000 words a day, when you need to do 3,000 to make a respectable living? It may be that you type too slowly to keep up with your mental rate of output. A typing course will boost your speed and accuracy and your ability to type figures. It may be that you dictate, but you are held up by the time it takes your typist to produce your copy, or by your old-fashioned dictation equipment. Think like a business and find a business-like solution: get a second typist, renew your investment in equipment.

Do you take hours to settle down in the morning, especially faced by a new job and sit at your desk tidying up your paperclips to avoid making a start? Take a time management course and try to understand why you are not coping better. If your research takes far too long because you do not know how to skip and skim and extract content rapidly, go on a speed-reading course. If it is your equipment that slows you down – an Amstrad that takes ages to respond to commands, for example – throw it out of the window and get hardware that helps, not hinders. If research takes too much of your time, be tough in restricting the range of the work you do to your specialist field. Get someone else to make the trips to the specialist library.

Are you over-perfectionist in your work, worrying about your semi-colons when the client is worrying about whether he (or she) is going to be able to tender for an order in time? Find out what the client wants and give it to him. He will be quite happy with write-in revisions of your work rather than a perfect reprint. Time is of the essence to him, and it is of the essence to you.

Be a bit of a bully − insist on help from the client or the agency. Offload to your client any work he can do as well as you − the information-gathering, the photocopying, telephoning the originator of the document with queries. Shed any work that might be better done by others: pay someone else to make the trip to the local library to check words, to proofread your work, to input a glossary in your computer. If you find a translation student or new translator to help you, you will be doing him or her a good turn as well.

Discover the benefits and rewards of job-sharing with a colleague with complementary expertise. If you like medical work but flounder in the pharmaceutical, find a soul mate with the opposite skills.

Pool the work that is better done as a group: marketing, for example.

SUMMARY

To sum up:
  (1) analyse and measure
     − yourself
     − the market
  (2) set goals
     − more money?
     − quality of working life?
and
  (3) act
     − get informed
     − get trained
     − get equipped
     − get help
  and a piece of advice you do not need, since you are members of ITI:
     − get together.

Improving the translator's lot

Florence Herbulot

Freelance translator

We are here, I gather, to try and find together some better ways of working and earning our living with translation. Better ways means faster ways, easier ways, more effective and also more profitable ways. I agree with Charles Polley when he says if you happen to know a wealthy translator, you can be pretty sure he or she did not get wealthy just by translating. We translate, day and night, and I for one am still waiting for wealth to come my way. . . . Nevertheless, I do try to make my work easier, faster, better, and to get paid more for it.

But let me first define the object of my talk: everything I will be saying refers to pragmatic translation, that is scientific, technical or semi-technical literature, and not literary work, which is another cup of tea, with other rules, and does not enter into the subject of this forum.

I think there are three main ways in which we can look for improvement:

(1) of course, the intellectual side of the job;
(2) and just as obvious, the mechanical side;
(3) the commercial aspect.

Now, just to confuse things a little, I'll jumble the order of these three subjects.

THE COMMERCIAL ASPECT

Translators must learn to sell their output. We are not naturally very good at that kind of thing, I must say, at least in a majority of cases: if we were, we would have other people working for us, and we would sell *their* output. But we can learn! What then are the main points which we must learn to improve?

- Providing better quotations, so as not to be taken in because we have given much too low a price.
- Knowing what price to ask for a job: if *we* don't know what we are worth, who does?
- Knowing when to send a job to a colleague, in good faith, and to which colleague: the one who will not kill the client for himself and for you.
- Knowing when to be suspicious of a client's willingness to pay, and how to collect payment in difficult cases.

– Knowing when to say *no*! And that is a tough one. We hate to turn down an offer, especially if we are freelancers with responsibilities and no security reserves. We must always have a little more work to do than we can cope with . . . and so we end up working all night, with results that could be better.

THE INTELLECTUAL SIDE

Two ways for improvement, here: trying to do better translations, and trying to do them faster.

Translating better

If you are *the* specialist in a subject, whatever that subject is, you are sure to be better than anyone else, to translate better, faster, and be able to get paid more. But the problem is that you can't always limit your activities to your specialist field. Take my case (sorry, but one always takes one's own case as an example): my speciality is sailing, and I do a reasonable amount of translation in that field, but it would not be enough to keep the wolf permanently from the door and keep my computer supplied. So I must work in other fields, where I may perhaps be less at ease, and in fact I have acquired a few other specialities.

Incidentally, and without questioning the truth of what Lanna Castellano told us about the necessity of being a specialist, I believe that translators do not need to be able to 'make' what they are translating about, they must simply know how to 'explain'. They must have a vast world knowledge, but it is not necessary that they be engineers or know as much about anything as an engineer does.

So, how can I improve my quality in those fields where I am a mere 'enlightened translator', but not a specialist? I think that research is the key word here. One must find out as much as possible about any subject before starting to translate, one must know what it is all about, and I don't mean in-depth preparation of the text itself – real problems do not appear anyway when you prepare a text, they have a habit of popping up later on, when you are translating proper – but collecting notions and concepts in the relevant literature, learning how a thing works, what it is called, how to speak about it. The language itself will not be a real difficulty once you know what it is all about, because you will be able to guess.

By the way, guessing is sometimes necessary even in one's speciality! Last year, I happened to translate a book on the America's Cup for publication in several European countries. The publisher was Italian, associated with other publishers in the various countries. The author was an Italian journalist, writing directly, chapter after chapter, while the yachts were racing in Australia, and sending her text over by fax to be translated on this side of the world. So far, no problems. But the journalist was in a great hurry, she never had time to proofread her text before faxing it, and what is more, she typed it on an old Olivetti portable which must have been around the world with her several times, and at some stage lost the letter 'c'. So the journalist would rapidly run through her chapter, once typed, and add some 'c's' here and there, mostly out of place, leaving a lot of gaps. The letter 'c' is very frequent in Italian. . . I can tell you that knowing what the story was, the main names, the main problems, helped me a lot when it came to guessing what she thought she had written! Another example: I was translating another book about sailing, and the author gave the length of some motor-boating races on the south coast of England, like Cowes–Torquay, but he gave them in kilometres. The United Kingdom was then deep in the throes of metrication, but sea races are given in miles, not kilometers, so I translated the figures. When they somehow did not fit, I had a doubt and finally found that the metrication process had been done on the wrong kind of miles: statute instead of nautical, which was silly because sailors never use statute miles. My publisher had the pleasure of sending a telex to the British publisher, emphasising that (1) metrication should not be pushed too far and (2) nautical and statute miles are not quite the same length.

Translating faster

This is also a condition for better living. I think it must come with experience. At first, being unsure of oneself, one doesn't dare go fast, fiddles endlessly with the text and looks for safety. A fellow translator in France, Pierre Duhem, has a theory he calls 'the bicycle theory': when cycling, the risk of falling down is far greater when going slowly. Going fast is a condition of safety. This seems to be true also for translation. If you go fast, there are many errors, many potholes in which you will not fall. You will jump over them, recover your balance, perhaps elude the difficulty, and then find the right solution later on, by inference. And by the way, it is much more effective to translate quickly, then let the job rest and take it up later: you will then see it with fresh eyes, as if it came from someone else, and everybody knows we are, oh, so much more intelligent when looking over someone else's work!

THE MECHANICAL SIDE

This is an area very much open to improvement, both qualitatively as well as in speed. I started translating on my family's Remington typewriter, like many of you I am sure, then I got a small portable which did me several books, and eventually got to IBM electric typewriters, of which I had three in succession, always with improved functions, such as the wonderful correction key. Word processing had come my way, but I was content to use other people's machines, until I got bored with having to wait for a moment when I would not be a bother to my friends. So I took the leap and bought a micro, an IBM PC XT – and spent two full weeks getting acquainted with the beast. I called him Stanislas and eventually got the better of him! Our relationship is now quite pleasant, thank you very much.

As regards speed, the progress from mechanical to electric typewriter, and then to micro, has been very profitable. Just as any typist can double his or her speed when changing from a mechanical to an electric typewriter, and go even further on a micro, a translator works faster when the mechanical obstacles are removed. No more backache, no more paper to change, no return at the end of each line, just concentrate on the brain work. I am no professional typist: I use only two fingers, I have to look at the keys, I make a lot of mistakes that have to be corrected afterwards, and yet I know that I can now translate about four or five pages an hour (on a subject in my speciality of course, where I have no, or almost no, research to do). On some other tough subjects, involving a lot of research, I might spend a full day doing three pages, as everybody does.

As regards the quality of the output, technical progress has also given us wonderful possibilities. With a word processor, you can correct every error. You can at last hope to reach near-perfection, even if it takes hours to perfect your editing and printing. No more correction fluid profusely spread on the pages, no more photocopying to conceal the correction fluid. We can provide beautifully typed pages, justified right and left, with proportional spacing, and looking very much like printed matter, but it is not always as easy or as fast as it sounds. However, I will give you a few tips that I have collected of late. For example, I found that it is much more profitable to do the corrections on a hard copy, a paper printout, then enter them on the floppy disc, before doing any editing. All other functions I do separately, one after the other: spell check, then layout, checking page ends, followed by a final general check of word-splitting, and so on. If I try to do several things at once, I am sure to forget some enormous mistakes that I only notice when the whole jolly thing is printed and ready to deliver! And that means it's back to the screen and printer for another hour or two, in the middle of the night, trying to get things right.

What I really want to say is that the main improvement, for me, came not from Stanislas but from the dictating machine. I did not choose it, it was forced onto me. Some years ago, I was hired to translate the projects submitted in English in an architecture contest. It was for the Centre Pompidou in Paris, and I can tell you that the final choice was not mine! But there were worse propositions. The organisers had launched their contest in two languages, French and English, and recruited one translator, me, thinking they would have a few contestants in English. Gradually, as projects arrived, we had to multiply: from one to three, then eight, and finally thirteen translators, all working in the same big hall and producing, very, very quickly, good quality texts to be typed also very quickly by a pool of ten or twelve typists. We worked for twenty-eight days, non-stop, from 9am to midnight, we translated some two or three thousand pages of esoteric literature, and after that we all went on holiday. Needless to say we could not do it by hand, it would have been too slow, or type it, it would have been too noisy. So we had to dictate: we were given machines, with small discs, and left to our own devices! For most of us it was quite new, and the first few hours were a bit difficult, then it started to get better. We went much faster, which was essential, and we also found that our output was of better quality, I mean more fluent, more readable, because it had passed the ear check, even if we had to whisper into our respective microphones. So it has been dictation for me, ever since. And it still is, despite Stanislas.

If I dictate, I must have someone to type for me, and pay for the typing: but I found that when I dictate, my output can be double what it is when I work directly on the word processor, for instance, so that takes care of the financial aspect. As I told you, the result is generally better, except perhaps for terribly down-to-earth and repetitive texts, technical manuals, or standards, for example, because repetitions don't stick to the ear as they do to the eye. On the other hand, as I have rather a visual type of memory, I tend to be much more critical of a translation I have not written or typed, but simply dictated, because when it comes back to me in typed form it is like someone else's text. My typist works at her home. She had an IBM with the same characters as mine, so I could do the corrections myself. Now she also has an IBM PC, she enters the translation and gives me the floppy disc for correcting, editing and printing. With this system, I almost never do the dictating and the editing on the same day, but usually with one or two days' interval.

To give you a few examples, I have done some timing on various translations I have done recently. These were all translations that I could do using my Harraps and my Robert, which are always on my table, close by, without having to search deep in other documents. And I did not count printing in the timing, because it can be done separately or while working on something else. But first I must explain that the billing unit in France is the typed page of translation, A4, double spacing, with about thirty lines of sixty characters or spaces, which represents a maximum of about 300 words, and more usually some 250–280. *Ils sont fous, ces Gaulois!*

Translation on the word processor

Twenty pages of text for an industrial technical magazine, installation of an electric cable between Sicily and the mainland. A little geology, a little geography, not much electricity, and a ready source of technical terms: the client wanted a well-written text to publish. It took me all day, 9 or 10 hours, and I was exhausted. I think it is my physical limit.
Average: 2 pages per hour.

Dictation and editing

Newspaper article about Hong Kong and its future. Easy to understand, not so easy to render.
9 pages. 2 hours translation, 1 hour editing.
Average: 3 pages per hour.

Big report on Videotex for a major international congress. Rather well written, so easier to translate, and with few terms that I had not met lately.
39 pages. 5 hours translation, 4½ hours editing.
Average: 4.1 pages per hour.

Report on the laying of electric cables with optical fibres. Also a text on a subject I had met lately, and which needed a good rendering in French, for publication.
27 pages. 4½ hours translation, 3¾ hours editing.
Average: 3.25 pages per hour.

Interview of an American skipper on sailing matters and the next America's Cup.
9.5 pages. 1¼ hour translation, 1 hour editing.
Average: 4.2 pages per hour.

The last item is really my speciality, the kind of subject I can translate even with an enormous bout of flu, but I know that if I do it directly on Stanislas it would take me about two hours translating (my limit is about four or five pages an hour), and even then I would not be rid of it without spending almost an hour on editing.

In short, dictation has given me a factor 2 in translation speed, and allows me to produce work which sounds much better: you never know, in fact, when you translate a report, if it is not going to be read aloud at a conference. On the other hand, thanks to word processing my translations look much better. But my target is always the same: getting more pay for my work! As I suppose it is also yours, I hope we can now have a lively discussion about all that.

Session 6: Report of discussion

Rapporteur: Rob Williams, freelance translator

Little time was left for discussion at the end of the Translators' Forum. However, a number of interesting points were raised, mostly concerning the benefits and drawbacks of word processors, now used by the vast majority of translators (although Florence Herbulot remarked that translators in France had been much slower to invest in word processing equipment).

COMPATIBILITY

Commenting on Lanna Castellano's paper, Claude Fleurent (May & Baker) said that, speaking in his capacity as a commissioner of translations, and he believed his view was fairly general in industry, he found it difficult to accept work not produced on IBM compatible equipment. Nothing else, he claimed, was acceptable to industry. Freelances investing in hardware should make sure it was IBM compatible. Lanna Castellano replied that since he was a work provider this was a reasonable comment. But would he pay for her equipment? If not, she would work for someone else instead.

Bill Masen (Interlingua-TTI), representing a translation company which is a major work provider, echoed Claude Fleurent's plea. IBM compatible equipment was certainly the best to buy.

George Varcoe (a Canadian translator based in Sweden) took issue with Lanna Castellano over her rejection of the need to offer compatibility. He argued that if clients wanted us to provide our translations on IBM compatible diskettes, we had to make the necessary investments to do so. Otherwise we stood to lose our clients. She agreed with him that the translator had to have the best tools available.

Claude Fleurent followed up his previous statement by pointing out that his company was quite willing to pay a higher fee if the work could be provided on floppy discs which it could use. The rate charged was not the major criterion in selecting freelances.

John Hayes, who for many years had argued against the need for word processors, said that he was still opposed to them. Translators did not save money by using them, and it actually took longer to produce work on a word processor. His riposte to Claude Fleurent was that no one was going to tell him what equipment to buy. IBM might be what clients want today, but what would it be tomorrow? He lived with these machines under sufferance. He had, though, acquired word processing equipment in order to satisfy some of his clients. He had bought Amstrads, and was already onto his fifth word processor. Lanna Castellano amused the audience by telling John that one of his greatest charms was that he changed his mind every year. He had now taken to using the Amstrad – what would it be next year? (These comments prompted Florence Herbulot to wonder what Lanna had had for breakfast!)

Eyvor Fogarty (freelance) suggested that John Hayes should think about Apple rather than IBM – plenty of clients wanted Apple compatibility.

PROOFREADING

Bill Masen drew attention to a danger of word processors. As a work provider, he had found that work was sometimes less well checked when produced on a word processor, because of the temptation simply to glance at the screen and not proofread the printed output. His view might be controversial, but he found that there had in some ways been an increase in carelessness.

Lanna Castellano agreed that errors had crept in. But did he inform translators when he found that their work had not been properly proofread? She was assured that this was indeed the case.

Florence Herbulot pointed out that in our obsession with the appearance of our work, it was easy to forget that it is the content that counts.

Catherine Muller (Taalwerk-Textperts BV, Netherlands) said that accurate typing was important. We tended to forget that more and more work now went straight to the printers. The text had to be flawless, and sloppy typing was unacceptable.

Eyvor Fogarty agreed with Florence Herbulot that it was far easier to spot errors on the printed copy, however clear the text might be on the screen.

Bruno Berger (West Germany) felt that one should not work too hastily. As Philip of Spain had said to one of his servants, 'Dress me slowly – I'm in a hurry!'

EYESTRAIN

Eyvor Fogarty also drew attention to the problem of eyestrain caused by working on word processors. Bruno Berger commented that a great deal of research had been carried out in West Germany to find the best screen configuration for minimising eyestrain. Tests had shown that black on white was easier on the eyes than green or amber on black. Florence Herbulot replied that she found amber on black to be less tiring, but that screen colour was more or less a matter of personal preference.

SPECIALISATION

There was considerable interest in the specialist/generalist debate. Gery Bramall noted that Florence Herbulot's specialist subject of sailing was even more abstruse than her own, opera libretti. Some translators had to be generalists simply because there was not enough work around in their specialisation. She was interested to hear Florence Herbulot emphasise the importance of research. Generalists had to do this all the time, and it was a very time-consuming task.

Barbara Snell (freelance) was consoled to hear that there was still space for the generalist. However, she disagreed with Lanna Castellano's comment that young translators should start by being generalists and gradually specialise as they acquired experience. She found it better to start in a fairly narrow field and get to know that field well – there would be plenty of variety even while specialising.

Rossana Basilico (Italy) said that she was very concerned about specialisation. It was essential to specialise in two or three subjects, her own being economics and finance, and it was important to work with specialists. Lanna Castellano replied that she quite agreed, one should marry a specialist, have friends and lovers who were specialists, choose godchildren who were going to be specialists – an extended family could be very useful. Florence Herbulot argued that we were involved in teamwork all the time. Life would be sad if we did not talk to each other.

OTHER POINTS

A number of other aspects were touched on. Eyvor Fogarty suggested that what translators should be aiming for was SPQR – small profit, quick return, to which Lanna Castellano replied that we could go for BPQR – big profit, quick return. The questioner also pointed out that translators suffered from an erratic workload, which was typical of all industry, but were fortunate in that they did not have to pay staff during slack times. This spare time should be used to talk to the taxman. Lanna Castellano replied that Eyvor Fogarty was not typical. She translated from minority languages, whilst most translators, working from the more common languages, were permanently overloaded and did not have time to talk to the taxman.

Florence Herbulot said that 20 per cent of her clients provided 80 per cent of her profit. However, the less profitable clients were friends, so she could not drop them!

Bruno Berger accepted that translators were responsible for the mistakes they made themselves, but argued that they could not be made responsible for errors made by the end-user of the translation.

Gery Bramall asked Florence Herbulot whether her clients were willing to wait for the time it took to have her dictated translations keyed in, returned from the typist, amended and printed, and what did she do while waiting for the work to come back? The reply was that they were willing to wait, and that she would usually be doing research on the next job. There were always several jobs on the go at once – it was a case of trying to plug holes with her fingers.

The sea of hands indicated that this lively discussion could have continued all afternoon. However, the tea break was already overdue, and Charles Polley brought the session to a close by thanking the speakers for their stimulating contributions.

Session 7: Interpreters' forum

Chaired by Roger Fletcher

Session 7: Report of forum

Rapporteur: Helena Bayliss, freelance interpreter and translator

The session took the form of questions and answers, occasionally breaking into heated discussion, but generally suffering from lack of time. A panel, comprising Christiane Driesen and Liese Katschinka, was available to deal with matters arising from papers given during a previous session, at which there had unfortunately been no time for questions.

Roger Fletcher suggested that it would be better to concentrate on standards, qualifications and training, and leave the questions of rates and remuneration till the latter half of the session. Questions then followed to Christiane Driesen.

Valerie Anderson: Who decides whether interpreting in court should be consecutive or whispered, and are any time limits imposed for an interpreter undertaking such work?
    Christiane answered that it was entirely up to the interpreter to choose the most appropriate technique in accordance with circumstances, and that it was quite in order to ask respectfully for a rest, or for better working conditions.

Claire Kahtan: What had been done in Hamburg to improve the standard of court interpreters and their recruitment?
    Christiane explained about the work of her association in educating the police and local authorities regarding the function of interpreters. She said that German thoroughness was an asset, they took her advice seriously especially after she had become *Frau Doktor*, and had organised meetings with police chiefs, courses in police academies, etc.

Santiago Ribeiro, AIIC, European Parliament: Who pays for interpreter's equipment in the courtroom, and how does one become a sworn interpreter?
    Christiane: If the trial is important, e.g. a Nazi trial, and if there are many witnesses and defendants, it is not difficult to persuade the authorities to hire equipment for simultaneous interpreting. A community interpreter could not cope with such trials, it was essential to be a qualified conference interpreter. To be 'sworn', it was necessary to pass very rigorous written and oral examinations, which tested knowledge of legal vocabulary in addition to interpreting techniques.

Roger Fletcher: The vast majority of court interpreters in Britain are self-

taught, as no training courses exist for those languages most in demand.
    Christiane's advice was for the setting up of training courses.

Philip Smith, AIIC: Do court interpreters work alone?
    Christiane pointed out that with a team of interpreters, whispering might become a problem.

Roger Fletcher: Should such interpreters be trained?
    Claire Kahtan: They require a thorough grasp of their two languages and cultures, a university degree and experience of life in general. Some formal legal training was obviously helpful, but one could be an excellent court interpreter, entirely self-taught.

Mansour Awad, France, told us that court interpreters on his country were considered legal experts – highly respected, and highly paid! He also said that a knowledge of legal terms in both languages was essential, as legal dictionaries were of little use.

Helena Bayliss then tried to steer the discussion out of the courtroom into the world of liaison interpreting, asking her colleagues, none of whom she had encountered professionally, how they would react under particular circumstances involving ethical questions.
    Roger Fletcher agreed that working with other interpreters, hired by the same client, but less competent than oneself, could give rise to problems – he once drew a judge's attention to another interpreter's mistake.
    Jamila Bernat, 'Just Words' (Arabic) also conceded that it was sometimes difficult to adhere strictly to the business of interpreting and not become involved with what was going on. She quoted an example where two sisters had been given English names to facilitate a court hearing. This greatly distressed the girls' mother, who was unable to follow the proceedings, and Jamila was forced to intercede. Jamila felt the need for a link between court interpreter and client; someone who could provide specialised background material, such as that relating to the Moslem religion, for example, where she herself would be unable to do so.

Miguel Costa Gomez, European Parliament, referring to Liese Katschinka's paper on the future of interpreting, wondered how new interpreters entered the profession.
    Liese explained that, during the summer term, she asked her teaching colleagues to recommend a promising college graduate. Indeed, that was how she herself came into the business.

Jane Hanstock, Salford University, said that everyone was concerned about standards and the problem of bad interpreters. Finding better trained people would help, but in the field of community interpreting this might be too optimistic – perhaps ITI could start a 'guardian angel' scheme for interpreters.

Liese Katschinka told the forum about just such a scheme, which had been operating in Austria for the last seven or eight years. During the summer, experienced interpreters invited students to understudy them in the booth, to follow the conference and perhaps take over the microphone for a half hour stint themselves. Such days of training were counted as interpreting experience when young people came to join AATI. Unfortunately, the scheme was not always very popular with the students, who preferred to sneak off to the beach rather than spend the whole day in a booth. As a result their report sheet would not be endorsed, and this inevitably led to repercussions.

Aziza Molyneux-Berry agreed that it was natural to be apprehensive about going to work in court for the first time, and volunteered to allow young interpreters to understudy her.

Then followed some examples of the serious problems sometimes encountered by court interpreters; a judge had once asked 'Madame Interpreter' (Aziza) to be quiet, and when she protested that it was her duty to tell the defendant what was going on, the instruction was to 'tell him later!' Interpreters had to be very patient and diplomatic – perhaps training courses for the judges would be a good idea.

Eduardo Perez, USA, told the forum about the training scheme currently operating in the state of New York. In the last three years, the authorities had recognised that court interpreters required training in order to cope with the wide range of terminology, etc. To work in a Federal Court, one now had to take a written examination and oral test, which assessed one's familiarity with different interpreting techniques.

Claire Kahtan asked about the qualifications of those giving such training in New York, and wondered whether instruction was available in languages other than Spanish – in Britain it was necessary to train people in thirty languages.

Eduardo Perez: There were 114 full-time court interpreters for Spanish in New York State alone and, to cope with a population of whom thirty million spoke only Spanish, the authorities spent most of their budget in training English/Spanish interpreters – one could of course be trained in other languages at one's own expense. In California, training in five or six languages was officially subsidised.

Jamila Bernat asked for guidance in respect of fees and wondered whether £25 per hour was too much to charge when interpreting for a solicitor.

Roger Fletcher replied that £14 per hour was his fee for Chinese, that AIIC's recommended rate for Government Institutions was £120 per day, and that the Lord Chancellor's paper recommended £8.50–£16 per hour, depending upon the language involved.

Maryline Neuschwander appealed to the forum not to forget that many conference interpreters were not members of AIIC and did not work in court.

She suggested that a network or forum which would encompass not only court, but all conference and liaison interpreters, be organised within ITI.

Florence Mitchell, Helena Bayliss and many others supported this idea.

Philip Smith called upon his colleagues not to reinvent the wheel, reminding them that AIIC had existed for thirty-five years.

Erica Lutterkort reported that the European Patent Office welcomed those working from French and German into English.

Biographical notes

Dr Keith Adkins
Senior Lecturer in Computing and Mathematics at the College of Ripon and York St John. He has worked on the adaptation of a software package for multilingual wordprocessing in the Department of Modern Languages at the University of Salford and is currently writing a book on Assembly Language programming.

Heinrich Allissat MITI
Served in the German Navy as a radar operator during the Second World War, and was a prisoner of war until 1948. Worked at various jobs until 1951 when he began translating at the US naval base at Bremerhaven. In 1952, joined Fried. Krupp, Essen, as translator and interpreter, and was appointed Head of Language Services there in 1976. He has been FIL since 1963, and joined the ITI as a founder member in 1986.

Valerie Anderson BA Hons, AIIC, MIL, MITI
Born Lima, Peru, Conference Interpreter since 1971, working for the UN and its Specialised Agencies, the EEC, inter-governmental organisations, non-governmental organisations, HMG. After university, spent seven years in the Foreign Office, then four years teaching in Lagos, Nigeria. On returning to the UK, worked as an ad hoc interpreter for the Foreign Office, British Council and tourist agencies, as well as freelance translating, before attending the Post-Graduate Conference Interpreting Course at the Polytechnic of Central London.

Dr Marie-Josée Andreasen
Translator in the medical and pharmaceutical areas (Fr–Sp–Port–It), with BA and MA degrees at Cambridge. Currently working in the Pharmaceutical Division of the Brussels-based company UCB SA, she divides her time between Brussels and Cambridge.

Helena Bayliss MITI
Born 1961 in USSR, studied Arts and Languages at Hertzen Pedagogical Institute, Leningrad. Resident in England since 1982, following marriage to English engineer. Postgraduate Diploma in Technical and Specialised Translation after year's full-time course at Polytechnic of Central London; now Member of Institute of Linguists and founder member of Institute of Translation and Interpreting. Currently operating as freelance interpreter, translator and language tutor, with major industrial clients and numerous contacts in arts and media. Interests include arts, music, literature and horse riding.

David Beattie MPhil., MITI.
Founder member of ITI. Staff translator with Hoechst UK Ltd since 1973, specialis-
ing in medicine, pharmaceutical science, pharmacology, life sciences. Co-organiser of
Medical Translation Workshops since 1985. Interests: Arthurian romance, half-
marathons, lexicography, Victorian glassware and earthenware, walking in the
Yorkshire Dales. Married, with one son.

Norman Boakes
Managing Director of Euro Marketors Parnership Ltd, he is a Fellow of the Institute of
Marketing and the Institute of Management Consultants, and also a Fellow of the
Royal Society of Arts. Trained originally as an engineer, he became a Sales Manager in
the agricultural chemicals industry before joining Nestlé where he spent thirteen years
and gained international sales and marketing experience in the United Kingdom,
Switzerland and Australia. In 1980 he was elected National Chairman, Institute of
Marketing, has been Vice Chairman, National Marketing Education Board and
adjudicates on the National Marketing Awards. He is also a Council Member of the
Institute of Management Consultants.

Christopher Burdon
Born in Stockton-on-Tees. Brought up in Middlesbrough. University years spent
mainly in Reading, with periods in Strasbourg and Saarbrücken. 1970 began teaching
French and German at Haberdashers' Askes Elstree, and continued as head of
department at Kettering Grammar and its successor, Kettering Boys School (comprehensive). Since 1980 staff translator at the General Secretariat of the EC Council of
Ministers, Brussels. Ensnared by the computerised terminology project in 1986: now
an enjoyable obsession. Interests: music, hi-fi, theology and my Brussels 'local'.

Dimity Castellano
Dimity Castellano has been looking after the interests of translators and interpreters
since 1970 when she joined the Institute of Linguists. In 1973 she took over administration of the Translators' Guild, leaving that only in 1986 to become Secretary of the ITI.
She has one Italian husband, two cats and ten canaries.

Lanna Castellano
Born in England, studied in England and France. Worked in NATO in Paris, Naples
and London; now works as a freelance translator in the legal field. Member of ITI
Council, with special interest in translation standards, cooperation and easing the
transition between university and working life, as well as professional development for
practitioners.

Patricia Crampton
Freelance translator. Read German and French at Oxford. Lived for periods in Sweden
and Mexico. Worked first as translator/reviser, Nuremberg Trials, then as head of
language department, BAT, and as abstracts journal editor, Woodall-Duckham Co.
Conference and language coordinator, NATO Parliamentarians, until marriage in
1959. Subsequently freelance translator, especially for medical subjects. Now mainly
book translator, with special interest in children's literature in developing world.
Winner of various literary awards.

Michael N. Croft
Open Exhibitioner in Modern Languages at Brasenose College, Oxford. Appointed to
a lectureship in French at Bath University in 1966, assisting in the development of the

pioneering course in translating and interpreting before becoming Director of Postgraduate Studies in 1974. Interests in nineteenth century French literature as well as in the training of linguists.

Melanie Dean
Studied modern languages at Salford University and was awarded a BA (Hons) in French and German in 1984. After graduation, she worked for one year as a management trainee for one of the major clearing banks. Melanie is now a staff translator with Rhône-Poulenc Ltd, in Dagenham, Essex. She is an Associate Member of the Institute of Translation and Interpreting, and Secretary of the Aslib Technical Translation Group.

Christiane-Jacqueline Driesen
Born in Paris. Took degree in German and Mediaeval Studies. Lived both in Hamburg and Paris since 1968. Attended courses on the French and German legal systems. Took doctorate at the Sorbonne Nouvelle (ESIT). Subject: 'Interpretation in the Criminal Courts of the FRG'. Freelance court interpreter and conference interpreter since 1976. Realising from practical experience in court interpreting the need for reform, became active on the board of BDÜ-Hamburg and Schleswig-Holstein, with a view to improving court interpretation by introduction of a new law and reformed examination.

Roger Fletcher
Roger Fletcher is a full-time freelance whose working time is divided between translation of technical and commercial documents from Chinese in the comfort of a modern electronic office and interpreting in Cantonese in such venues as police stations, prisons and courts. The amount of time spent on each is more a function of market forces than of personal preference.

Michael L.N. Forrest
Mechanical Sciences Tripos and post-graduate research in solid state electronics at Trinity College Cambridge. Joined The British Tabulating Machine Company ('Hollerith') in 1957 as an electronics engineer. BTM formed part of ICT and subsequently ICL and STC. Responsibilities in the areas of Computer Engineering (1961–64), Manufacturing (1964–65) and Sales (1965–66) within ICT. On formation of ICL in 1967 responsible for planning of the product line of the merged company and subsequently for all system software development for the new product line. 1974–75 responsible for all internal systems of ICL. In 1976 moved to headquarters of ICL's European Division in Paris responsible for Marketing, Services and Finance. 1981 moved back to the United Kingdom as Director of Business Operations responsible for analysis of Sales forecasts and determination of the Company's manufacturing programme. From 1986 Director of Operations, ICL International (and subsequently ICL Europe), now responsible to the President of ICL Europe for day to day HQ supervision of operational performance in continental Europe.

John Gardam
Graduated from London University in 1956 with a 2nd Class Honours Degree in Mechanical Engineering, and joined BR at Swindon Locomotive Works. In 1962 he moved to Utrecht, Holland, for work for ORE, the research organisation of the International Union of Railways. Since returning to the United Kingdom, four years later, he has held a number of engineering posts with BR both in Glasgow and in Derby. He is a part-time freelance translator and author.

Alan James Gilderson
Born in Belfast, Northern Ireland in 1931. Modern and Medieval Languages Tripos, Cambridge, 1951–54. FIL 1962–86, MTG 1963, MITI 1987. Administrative staff of former London County Council 1954–60. Emigrated to Sweden 1960. Staff translator Alfa-Laval 1960–63, sales promotion editor 1963–66. Copywriter STB Stockholm 1966–69. Copywriter Anderson & Lembke Stockholm and Helsingborg 1969–87. Copy director BBI Helsingborg 1987 – . Part-time freelance translator since 1962.

John D. Graham
Born Scotland 1939, BA in French, German and Russian London University. Founder Member of ITI. Fellow of the Institute of Linguists since 1967. After several years at Tube Investments in Birmingham, joined Mannesmann Demag in Duisburg, Germany, in 1973. Deputy head of the Central Translation Services there from 1975, became Head of Department in 1980. Actively involved in just about everything connected with translation and translators (Regional Secretary/Chairman BDÜ Duisburg; General Secretary of International Association Language & Business; member of the Koordinierungsausschuss Praxis und Lehre (BDÜ) and also in the Institute of Linguists West German Regional Society. Currently lecturing part-time at the University of Duisburg (Translation for non-translators).

Dr Florence Herbulot
Technical and literary translator (ninety published books and several thousand pages of technological literature) with many interests and one strong speciality – sailing. Maître de Conférences de l'Université Paris III. In charge of the Translation Section at E.S.I.T. (Ecole Supérieure d'Interprètes et de Traducteurs de l'Université Paris III). Past President of the S.F.T. (Société Francaise des Traducteurs).

Liese Katschinka
Freelance conference interpreter and sci-tech translator, court interpreter and translator. Born in Vienna, graduate of University of Vienna (interpreting and translation), member of Österreichischer Übersetzer- und Dolmetscherverband 'Universitas' since 1968, member of A.I.I.C. since 1976 (A: German, B: English, C: French), Secretary General of Österreichischer Übersetzer- und Dolmetscherverband 'Universitas' since 1984, Secretary of Organising Committee for the Xth World Congress of FIT, Vienna, 1984, FIT Vice-President between 1984 and 1987, Chairman of FIT Interpreters' Committee since 1984.

Hugh Keith
After studying French and German at Oxford and working at a German university, Hugh Keith trained as a teacher at York University. He now works as a lecturer in German at Heriot-Watt University, Edinburgh and helps run Integrated Language Services, the university translation and interpreting service to industry and commerce. He has himself worked extensively as a freelance translator and interpreter, both in Britain and Germany. He is a member of the ITI education and training committee.

Jean Kirby
Jean became a freelance translator after working for some years as a dairy bacteriologist both in England and Denmark. She is on the Board of the TG and is a member of the ITI Council.

Valerie Landon
Began her professional life as a translator, but over the last decade demand for interpreting has increased to such an extent that this part of her work tends to

predominate. Works as a freelance for government, industry and commerce. Is principally engaged in conference interpreting, both consecutive and simultaneous, but as the occasion requires works also in ad hoc situations, and has even been known to interpret the odd after-dinner speech.

Robert David MacDonald
Associate Director of the Citizens Theatre, Glasgow, for the last eighteen years, during which time, in addition to work as actor, director and musician, he has written twelve and translated forty plays for the company from six languages. His most recent work includes translation of Racine's Phèdre (Aldwych Theatre, London 1986), Molière's L'Ecole des Femmes (National Theatre, London 1987) Lorca's La Casa de Bernarda Alba (Lyric Theatre, London 1987) and both parts of Goethe's Faust, currently playing at the Lyric Theatre, Hammersmith.

Pamela Mayorcas
Took the Polytechnic of Central London's Diploma in Modern Languages and European Studies 1965–68. Her first job was with the Iron and Steel Institute. In 1970 she joined the Foreign Office team which translated the authentic English texts prior to UK accession to the EC. Since 1973, she has worked for the EC Commission, starting as a technical translator; but currently concerned with information and documentation systems for translators. Was awarded an MSc in Information Science by the City University in 1981. Is specially interested in information problems as they apply to translators, including the use of information technology, and has published a number of articles on the subject. Has been actively involved with ITI since its inception.

Ewald Osers
One of the best-known translators in the world today. Ewald Osers has been a tireless worker for the Institute and has served in many organisations both national and international. He has translated over ninety books, and has received prizes and distinctions too numerous to mention, but was especially proud to be elected a Fellow of the Royal Society of Literature in 1984.

Charles Polley
Before becoming a translator Chas Polley held various management jobs, followed by fourteen years in computer sales. He began in technical translation about four years ago, going full-time as a freelance in 1985. He has a BA in Modern Languages and the Diploma in Management Studies, and is a Member of BIM and Fellow of the Institute of Data Processing Accountants. As an Associate of the ITI he is a member of its Translators' Activities Committee, and is co-founder and Chairman of the North-West Translators' Network.

Guyonne Proudlock
Guyonne Proudlock was born in Paris in 1950 and educated in France and England. She has been a freelance translator for twelve years and has also been a teacher of translation at postgraduate level. More recently she has taken up research at Stirling University alongside her translation work, in the field of machine translation. She is particularly interested in the analysis of human translation, computer-assisted translation and fully automatic translation as a man-machine system.

Juan Sager
Studied in Argentina, USA, Scotland and Federal Republic of Germany, Professor of Modern Languages and Head of Department of Language and Linguistics and Centre

for Computational Linguistics (CCL) at the University of Manchester Institute of Science and Technology. Chairman of the EC Commission's Advisory Committee of Experts on Transfer of Information between Languages (CETIL).

Ros Schwartz
Ros Schwartz lived in Paris for eight years and is now a London-based freelance translator from French, Italian and Spanish. Specialising in literary translation and film subtitling, she runs workshops at Goldsmiths' College and is on the Executive Committee of the Translators Association. She was a consultant for the revised Robert/Collins dictionary and is a judge for the Scott Moncrieff prize.

Alastair M. Scouller
After qualifying at the University of Glasgow and the Polytechnic of Central London, he became an auxiliary staff interpreter at the EC, Brussels, in 1975, since which date he has also been a freelance conference interpreter. He became Senior Lecturer at PCL in 1986, and was involved with the Institute of Linguists' Community Interpreting Project as visiting tutor-examiner-adviser from 1986–88.

John A. Seager
Qualified in Spanish at the Universities of Leeds and Seville, and joined Bowater in 1960, moving to Courtaulds in 1969, Sperry in 1973, and Duracell Europe (then Mallory Batteries) in 1976. He has been their Senior Vice-President, Manufacturing and Technical Development, since 1981. He is trilingual (Eng–Fr–Sp), with a working knowledge of German, Italian, and Flemish. His mainly outdoor interests include shooting, fishing and 'other forms of conservation'.

Danica Seleskovitch
Director of the Sorbonne postgraduate school for conference interpreters and translators. She began her career as a conference interpreter with the French Embassy in Washington DC and the ECSC in Luxemburg. From 1956 onwards she worked as a freelance. In 1969 she joined Paris University where she now holds a professorship.

Mike Shields
Engineer-cum-freelance translator who started running industrial libraries some twenty-two years ago and has continued ever since. Now Chief Information Officer at the Motor Industry Research Association, he is a Fellow of the Institute of Information Scientists. He is also a widely published writer and poet, and is Editor of the literary magazine Orbis.

Jane Taylor
A graduate of Oxford University, she lectures in the Department of French Studies at Manchester University. She runs a successful third-year course in Translation Studies, with a practical and linguistic base. She is particularly committed to forging links between the practising translator and the academic world. Her own speciality is the translation of books on climbing and outdoor pursuits, primarily from French although she also handles Italian and German.

Albin Tybulewicz
Chartered physicist, scientific editor and freelance translator. Former Editor of Physics Abstracts; currently editing three cover-to-cover translation journals

published by the American Institute of Physics. Translated over sixty physics mono-graphs from Russian into English. Member of the Steering Group (which founded ITI) and now of the Council of ITI.

Hilde Watson
Hilde Watson has a long career as translator and full-time conference interpreter. She is working for international organisations, British industry and the Commission in Brussels. In the past she also worked as a teacher and is co-author of two commercial textbooks.

Rob Williams
After studying German and Danish at Cambridge University, took the Diploma in Technical and Specialised Translation at the Polytechnic of Central London. Went freelance in 1985 after six years as head of the translation section at the Defence Research Information Centre, Orpington. Translates from German, Dutch, Swedish, Danish, Norwegian and French, specialising in the life sciences, computers and aerospace. Outside interests include rugby (approaching the end of a less than glorious career), hill-walking, running and cinema.

E. Boris Uvarov
Born in Russia, 1910. Came to England in 1920. Read chemistry at Imperial College (Royal College of Science); awarded ARCS and BSc (Hons.Chem.) in 1930 and postgraduate diploma (DIC) in biochemistry in 1931. Science teacher, Beacon Hill School (under Bertrand and Dora Russell); technical manager of a food factory; senior chemistry teacher, Dartington Hall School and Taunton School; head of Technical Information Bureau, Courtaulds Ltd; freelance translator from 1954. Fellow of the Royal Institute (now Society) of Chemistry. Member of Aslib Council, Chairman of Aslib Conference and Meetings Committee and of Aslib Textile Group in early 1950s; sometime member of Aslib TTG. Co-author of *Penguin dictionary of science* (1st ed. 1942, 6th ed. 1986). Took part in revision of the *Callaham Russian/English dictionary* (2nd ed.) and contributed to Emin's *Russian/English physics dictionary*. Numerous papers at various conferences (Unesco, Aslib). Cover-to-cover translations of several Russian chemical journals and books since 1954.

Attendance list

Adkins, Dr Keith, College of Ripon and York St John, York
Aherne, Deirdre, Student, Leeds, West Yorkshire
Al-Hamid, Mr Abu-Bakr Muhsin, Student, Aden, P.D.R. of Yemen
Al-Khafaji, Mr M F, Student, Iraqi Translators' Association
Albano, Ms Maria Aurora, Freelance translator, Cambridge
Alexander, Mrs Jeanette, Freelance translator, London
Allissat, Mr Heinrich, Fried. Krupp GmbH, Essen, West Germany
Anderson, Ms Janet, Freelance translator, Orpington, Kent
Anderson, Mrs Valerie, Conference interpreter, London
Andersson, Mr Johan, David Knight & Co Språkkonsulter AB, Stockholm, Sweden
Andreasen, Dr Marie-Josée, UCB, Braine l'Alleud, Belgium
Ansah, Mrs Sara, Translator, London
Arbia, Ms G Nicoletta, Freelance translator, London
Arthern, Mr Peter, Head, English Translation Division, Council of the European
    Communities, Brussels, Belgium
Astwood, Mr Lorance, Department of Trade and Industry, London
Awad, Mr Mansour, Freelance translator/interpreter, Pithiviers, France
Babar, Mr Navid, Race Equality Unit, Sheffield City Council
Bacon, Josephine
Bailey, Ms Joy, First Edition, Cambridge
Baker, Robin
Ballard, Ms Catherine, Leeds Interpreting and Translation Service
Barefoot, Mr Brian, Freelance translator, Bradford-on-Avon
Basilico, Ms Rossana, Milan, Italy
Baston, Mr William, British Telecom Research Laboratories, Ipswich
Bayliss, Mrs Helena, London
Bell, Ms Maite, London Interpreting Project
Berger, Mr Bruno, Hannover, West Germany
Beria, Ms Anna, Commission of the European Communities, Brussels, Belgium
Bernat, Ms Jamila, Just Words (Arabic), London
Bird-Louis, Mrs M M, Freelance translator, Congleton, Cheshire
Boakes, Mr Norman, Euro Marketors Partnership
Bokx, Mr Hans, Freelance translator, Schiedam, The Netherlands
Bond, Mr Geoff, W S Atkins, Epsom, Surrey
Boothroyd, Mr Paul, InTra eG, Stuttgart, West Germany
Böse, Mrs Ursula, Heriot-Watt University, Edinburgh
Bradhering, Ms Hanna, Translingua, Bonn, West Germany
Bradley, Mrs Susie, Freelance translator, Welling, Kent
Braley, Mr Alan, Freelance translator, Knebworth, Hertfordshire
Bramall, Lady, Freelance translator, London

Breakwell, Mr Neil, Freelance translator, Hitchin, Hertfordshire
Brunner, Ms Susan, Interlingua TTI, London
Brusick, Ms Huguette, Société Française des Traducteurs, Paris, France
Burdon, Mr Christopher, Council of Ministers, Brussels, Belgium
Buxbom, Mrs Kirsty, Rank Xerox, Welwyn Garden City
Camugli, Mr Jean, International Coffee Organisation, London
Cardodo, Elena
Carr, Ms Myriam, University of Salford
Castellano, Mrs Lanna, Freelance translator, London
Chadwick, Mr Nicholas, Freelance translator, London
Charlton, Ms Carol, Dragonfly Communications, London
Clarke, Douglas, Cranfield Institute of Technology
Crampton, Mrs Patrica, Freelance translator, Calne, Wiltshire
Christodoulou, Ms Irina, Postgraduate student, University of Salford
Clark, Mr Robert, Freelance translator, Cambridge
Coke, Ms Elspeth, Electricity Council
Colby, Ms Fifolle, Freelance interpreter, London
Conrad, Ms Amanda, Freelance translator, Tunbridge Wells, Kent
Coveney, Professor James, Bell Educational Trust, Bath
Cowan, Ms Christine, University of Newcastle
Craddock, Mr John, Freelance translator, Maidenhead, Berkshire
Craven-Bartle, Mr Joseph, SpanText AB, Karlskoga, Sweden
Croft, Mr Michael, University of Bath
Cronin, Mrs Francine, Freelance translator/interpreter, London
Cross, Mr Graham, Freelance translator, Ewloe, Clwyd
Cynkin, Mr Christopher, Interverbum AB
Dahl, Mr Emilio, Freelance translator, Södertälje, Sweden
Dale, Ms Lorna, Metropolitan Police, London
Day, Mrs Rita, Freelance translator/interpreter, London
Dean, Ms Melanie, May & Baker Ltd, Dagenham, Essex
Dean, Mrs U M, Freelance translator, East Molesey, Surrey
Denby, Mr David, National Institute for Higher Education, Dublin
Dent, Ms Hannah, FCO, London
Depiante, Ms Nélida, Freelance translator, Farnborough, Hampshire
De Witt-Wijnen, Ms Ann, Lecturer, University of Groningen
Dewsnap, Mr Robert, Freelance translator, Sölvesborg, Sweden
Driesen, Ms Christiane-Jacqueline, Freelance interpreter, Hamburg, West Germany
Dumonteil-Lagrèze, François, Interlingua TTI, London
Dyson, Ms Evelyn, Commercial & Technical Translations, Lancaster
Eie, Mr Bernt, Centre for Industrial Research, Oslo, Norway
Eie, Mrs Eva, Freelance translator, Eiksmarka, Norway
Ellestad, Mr Everett, Intense HB, Tumba, Sweden
Evans, Mr Kenneth, Freelance translator, Murg-Hänner, West Germany
Everist, Mr Robert, Fried. Krupp GmbH, Essen, West Germany
Farrel, Mr B P, Molins plc, High Wycombe, Buckinghamshire
Fenner, Mr Andrew, Freelance translator, London
Fletcher, Mr Roger, Freelance interpreter, Royston, Hertfordshire
Fleurent, Mr Claude, May & Baker, Dagenham, Essex
Fogarty, Mrs Eyvor, Freelance translator, London
Forrest, Mr Michael, Vice President, ICL Europe, London
Fortune, Mrs Maud, Ciba-Geigy Pharmaceuticals, Horsham, West Sussex
Fraser, Ms Janet, Industrial Relations Services, London
Freibott, Mr Gerhard, Krupp Industrietechnik GmbH, Duisburg, West Germany

Gardam, Mr John, Railway Translation Service, Etwall, Derbyshire
Gibson, Mr Paul, ICI plc, London
Gilderson, Mr Alan, BBI Helsingborg, Sweden
Goddard, Mr Richard, Freelance translator, Romford, Essex
Goodman, Mr John, Transcommunications Ltd, Melton Mowbray, Leicestershire
Goodwin, Mrs Elena, IMO, London
Gosling, Mrs Uta, BSI, Milton Keynes, Buckinghamshire
Graham, Mr John D, Freelance translator, Duisburg, West Germany
Green, Ms Consuelo, Amnesty International, London
Griffin, Mr John, Freelance translator, Battle, East Sussex
Grönvall, Ms Karin, David Knight & Co Språkkonsulter AB, Stockholm, Sweden
Grütters, Ms Angela, International Business Forms Industries, Torquay, Devon
Habte, Ms Fekade, London Interpreting Project
Hadley, Mr Perry, David Knight & Co Språkkonsulter AB, Stockholm, Sweden
Hagemann, Mr Wolfgang, DIN, Berlin, West Germany
Hammond, Mrs Philippa, Freelance translator, Inverness, Scotland
Hanstock, Ms Jane, University of Salford, Manchester
Hargreaves, Ms Gillian, Freelance translator, Ruislip, Middx
Harris, David
Harris, Mrs Ulrike, GNI Ltd, London
Harrison, Ms Susan, Department of Trade and Industry, London
Harvey, Mr David, Freelance translator, Sunbury-on-Thames, Middlesex
Haydock, Ms Juliet, Freelance translator, Teddington, Middlesex
Hayes, Mr John, Hayes Engineering Services, Hertfordshire
Hayward, Mr Oliver, FCO, London
Hedegaard, Isolde
Henrickson, Ms Ann, W P Thompson & Co, Liverpool
Herbulot, Ms Florence, Freelance translator, Paris, France
Herrera, Mrs Hildegard, Condor Translation Services, Kingston-upon-Thames, Surrey
High, Mr Graeme, Freelance translator, London
Hind, Ms Margaret, Freelance translator, London
Hollow, Mr Mike, BBC Monitoring Service, Reading
Holmes, Ms Susan, Freelance translator, Brighton, East Sussex
Hooper, Dr Raymond, Boehringer Mannheim GmbH, West Germany
Howard, Mrs Gerda, Freelance translator, Bicester, Oxfordshire
Hutson, Mr John, Freelance translator, East Molesey, Surrey
Inches, Mr Robin, Editor, *ITI News*, Sherborne, Dorset
Ingleton, Mr Roy, Legal & Technical Translation Services, Maidstone, Kent
Jaeger, Ms Angelika, Freelance translator, Frankfurt, West Germany
James, Mr Martin, British Manufacture & Research Co Ltd, Grantham, Lincolnshire
Jelaska, Ms Rosana, Freelance translator, Lymington, Hampshire
Jenkins, Ms Susan, Leatherhead Food Research Association
Jensen, Mr J Klinth, European Parliament (retired)
Johns, Mr Michael, Volvo AB, Göteborg, Sweden
Jones, Mr Roger, Australia Post, NSW, Australia
Jutet, Ms Monique, Freelance translator, Asnières, France
Kahtan, Claire, London
Katschinka, Ms Liese, Chairman, FIT Interpreters' Committee, Vienna, Austria
Keigher, Ms Ginette, Tek Translation, London
Keith, Mr Hugh, Heriot-Watt University, Edinburgh
Kingscott, Mr Geoffrey, Editor, *Language Monthly*, Nottingham
Kirby, Mr Andrew, Lloyds Bank plc, London

Kirby, Mrs Jean, Freelance translator, Crawley, West Sussex
Klipstein, Mrs Freda, London
Knight, Mr David, David Knight & Co Språkkonsulter AB, Stockholm, Sweden
Knighton, Mr Paul, Freelance translator, Willingham, Cambridgeshire
Krone, Ms Elisabeth, Freelance translator, Berlin, West Germany
Landon, Mrs Valerie, Freelance interpreter, Pinner, Middlesex
Lebaut, Ms Geneviève, Paris, France
Lefebure, Mr Eric, Bank of England, London
Lessing, Walter
Lester, Ms Virginia, International Tanker Owners' Pollution Federation, London
Lew, Mrs Minna, Freelance interpreter, Bromley, Kent
Liepa, Mrs Philippa, Department of Trade and Industry, London
Lima, Ms Aud Martha, Nesøya, Norway
Lina-Flowers, Mrs Francoise, Freelance translator, Hampton Wick, Surrey
Lindner, Ms Annelies, Redland plc, Reigate, Surrey
Little, Ms Gwyn, Department of Trade and Industry, London
Lovell-Pank, Mr Martin, Freelance translator, London
Lutterkort, Mrs Erica, European Patent Office, Munich, West Germany
Macdonald, Mr Robert, Assistant Director, Citizens Theatre, Glasgow
McPhail, Mrs Helen, Freelance translator, Shrewsbury, Shropshire
Maddra, Mrs L J, Link Line Business Services, Hull
Magnusson Murray, Mrs Ulla, Consultant, Translation Management, Sawbridge-
    worth, Hertfordshire
Masen, Mr William, Interlingua TTI Ltd, London
Mauriello, Ms Gabriella, Freelance translator, Milan, Italy
Mayorcas, Ms Pamela, Commission of the European Communities, Brussels, Belgium
Mead, Mrs Annie, Freelance interpreter, West Wickham, Kent
Meak, Ms Lidia, University of Trieste, Italy
Meijlink, Mrs Jane, Freelance translator, Rockanje, The Netherlands
Mello, Ms Fernanda, Freelance translator, Milan, Italy
Millward, Ms Pamela, FCO, London
Minett, Mr Stanley, Freelance translator, Great Yarmouth, Norfolk
Misuri Charkham, Mrs Debbie, Freelance translator, London
Mitchell, Mrs Florence, Freelance translator, Richmond, Surrey
Mitler, Mr Louis, American Translators' Association, Charlottesville, Va., USA
Molyneux-Berry, Mrs Aziza, Freelance interpreter, London
Mountford, Ms Jane, Brixton Estate plc, London
Muller, Drs Catherine, Taalwerk Textperts b.v., Soest, The Netherlands
Napthine, Mrs Anne, Shell International Petroleum Co, London
Neuschwander, Ms Maryline, Freelance translator/interpreter, Southampton,
    Hampshire
Nock, Mrs Anne, Freelance translator, Epsom, Surrey
Oliver, Dr David, Oliver Translation Services, Leighton Buzzard, Bedfordshire
Orme, Ms Helen, Student, Nescot, Epsom, Surrey
Ortega, Ms Angela, Student, Polytechnic of Central London, London
Osers, Mr Ewald, Freelance translator, Reading, Berkshire
Paish, Mrs Myriam, Freelance translator/interpreter, Wimborne, Dorset
Pampanini, Ms Danila, Freelance translator, Harrow, Middlesex
Parker, Mrs Gisela, Freelance translator, Twickenham, Middlesex
Parker, Mr Roger, Freelance translator, Potters Bar, Hertfordshire
Paton, Mr James, Bergen Translatorbyrå, Skjoldtun, Norway
Pattison, Mrs Ann, Freelance translator, Sutton, Surrey
Percival, Mr Christopher, Flambard (European) Ltd, Durham City

Perez-Ravelo, Eduardo, American Translators' Association
Picken, Ms Catriona, Freelance translator, London
Politi, Ms Monique, University of Trieste, Italy
Polley, Mr Charles, Freelance translator, Huddersfield, West Yorkshire
Prentis, Simon
Price, Ms Penny, Freelance translator, Mitcham, Surrey
Proudlock, Mrs Guyonne, Freelance translator, London
Rayar, Ms Louise, University of Limburg, Maastricht, The Netherlands
Riboldi, Ms Paola, Freelance translator, Padua, Italy
Roberts, Mr David, Philips Research Laboratories, Redhill, Surrey
Rodriguez, Mrs Mary, Freelance translator, Estepona, Spain
Rogers, Ms Jenny, ICI Ltd, Middlesbrough, Cleveland
Rogers, Mrs Marion, Freelance translator, Kettering, Northamptonshire
Rosenbaum, Mr Peter, Freelance translator, Welwyn, Hertfordshire
Rössevold, Mr Björg, Freelance translator, Oslo, Norway
Ryder, Maria
Sager, Professor Juan, UMIST
Saleh, Mrs Thana, Freelance translator, London
Sanchez de Brennan, Mrs Pilar, Freelance translator/interpreter, Alderley Edge,
    Cheshire
Sant'iago Ribeiro, Mr Manuel, European Parliament, Brussels
Schamp, Mr E R, Transcommunications Ltd, Melton Mowbray, Leicestershire
Schenk, Dr Victor, Freelance translator, Bowdon, Cheshire
Schofield, Mrs Kerstin, Freelance translator, Abingdon, Oxfordshire
Scholl, Mrs U, Harderwijk, The Netherlands
Schorn, Mrs Maria, The Hague, The Netherlands
Schwartz, Ms Ros, Freelance translator, London
Scouller, Mr Alastair, Polytechnic of Central London
Seager, John, Duracell plc
Seleskovitch, Professor Danica, ESIT, Paris, France
Sharma, Mrs Rannheid, Freelance translator, Brentwood, Essex
Sharpe-Geuther, Mrs Aileen, Freelance translator, Berlin, West Germany
Shaw, Mr Martin, FCO, London
Shields, Mr Mike, Motor Industry Research Association
Smith, Mrs Marti, Freelance translator, Cobham, Surrey
Smith, Mr Philip, Conference interpreter, Sutton Coldfield, West Midlands
Smith, Mr R D, Freelance translator, Stockton-on-Tees, Cleveland
Snell, Miss Barbara, Freelance translator, Gloucester
Snelling, Mr David, University of Trieste, Italy
Soubrier, Ms Michèle, Rhône Poulenc Agrochimie, Lyons, France
Spalter, Mrs Vicky, Freelance translator, London
Starren, Mr P M G, State School of Translation, Maastricht, The Netherlands
Stellbrink, Mr Hans-Jürgen, Ruhrgas AG, Essen, West Germany
Stewart, Ms Susan, FCO, London
Stoker, Ms Julie, FCO, London
Stuart, Mr Gordon, Freelance translator, Arbroath, Angus, Scotland
Suschenko, Mrs Lisa, Freelance translator, London
Swoboda, Miss Anna, CBA Translations, Bristol
Sykes, John, Chairman, ITI, London
Symonds, Mr Robert, Freelance translator, Bromley, Kent
Synning, Mrs Margareta, Swedbank, Stockholm, Sweden
Talukdar, Ms Manize, Student, Harrow, Middx
Taylor, Dr Jane, University of Manchester

Tennenhaus, Ms Shula, Softrans International Ltd, Blackrock, Co. Dublin, Ireland
Thunecke, Dr J, Trent Polytechnic, Nottingham
Trandafilovic-Alvarez, Mrs Dragana, Freelance translator, London
Tsuji, Ms Mitsue, Freelance translator/interpreter, Birmingham
Türkistanli, Mr Ahmet, Freelance translator, London
Uvarov, Mr E Boris, Freelance translator and lexicographer, Stowmarket, Suffolk
Van Hoorn, Ms Annet, Student, University of Amsterdam, The Netherlands
Varcoe, Mr George, Global English Språkkonsulter AB, Osterskär, Sweden
Verpalen, Ms Elizabeth, University of Groningen, The Netherlands
Vitale, Mr Marc, Freelance translator, Paignton, Devon
Wagenpfeil, Mr Gerhard, Translingua, Bonn, West Germany
Walker, Ms Sally, Sally Walker Language Services, Bristol
Walsh, Ms Celia, International Business Forms Industries, Torquay, Devon
Walter, Dr Robert, Chemical Translation Services, High Wycombe,
    Buckinghamshire
Wariwoda, Ms Loisa, David Knight & Co Språkkonsulter AB, Stockholm Sweden
Watanabe, Ms Syozo, East Grinstead, West Sussex
Watson, Mrs Hilde, Freelance interpreter, London
Watts, Mrs Niki, Freelance translator, Huntingdon, Cambridgeshire
Watts, Mr Quentin, Huntingdon, Cambridgeshire
Weeks, Mr David, Freelance translator, Farnham, Surrey
Welsing, Drs W P B M, State School of Translation, Maastricht, The Netherlands
Wenkert, Mr George, Freelance translator, London
Weston, Mrs Diana, Freelance translator, London
Wickens, Dr Henry, Council of Europe, Strasbourg, France
Williams, Mr Rob, Freelance translator, London
Willson, Mrs Debbie, Hayes Engineering Services, Croxley Green, Hertfordshire
Wilson, Mrs Barbara, FCO, London